James Laxer

CANADA'S ENERGY CRISIS

James Lorimer & Company,
Publishers
1975

ISBN paper 0-88862-087-X
      cloth 0-88862-088-8

Cover design by Michael Constable
Design by Lynn Campbell
Author photo by Paul Craven

James Lorimer & Company, Publishers
35 Britain Street
Toronto Canada

Printed and bound in Canada

Canadian Shared Cataloguing in Publication Data

Laxer, James, 1941-
    Canada's energy crisis / James Laxer.

1. Petroleum industry and trade—Canada.
2. Power resources—Canada. 3. Energy
policy — Canada. I. Title.

HD9574.C22L382   338.4'7'66550971
ISBN: 0-88862-088-8; 0-88862-087-X (pbk.)

To Krista

Acknowledgements

I wish to express my gratitude to Anne Forrest for her valuable research work in the preparation of this book. Her contribution of ideas and critical comments was of great assistance. I also wish to thank Jim Lorimer for his helpful criticisms and encouragement during the writing of this book.

James Laxer
Toronto
March 1974

Contents

1   Introduction

To many Canadians the energy crisis appears as a sudden and inexplicable threat to the bountiful supply of energy that we have come to take for granted. What we see is the surface of the crisis, the baffling and incongruous events occurring daily on both the international and national scenes.

Some of these have been merely puzzling: conflicting reports of energy hoarding (by suppliers) and shortages side by side in the U.S. press; the Arab oil boycott, ostensibly aimed at the U.S., which posed a far more serious threat to the Japanese and the Europeans than to the Americans; Mitchell Sharp's inability to find out whether Canada was included on the boycott list of the Arab countries.

However, the energy crisis has not only been puzzling people, but it has been scaring them as well. Many have seen it as a signal that the world is entering an age of scarce resources. People fear that the future of industrial societies is now threatened by the sheer limits of the earth itself. In this vein Prime Minister Pierre Trudeau has warned Canadians that objectives like full employment and higher living standards may be unrealistic. The appearance of worsening shortages of energy in the industrialized nations since 1970 has lent credence to the view that physical shortages of energy resources can now be regarded as a fact of life.

This book rejects the interpretation that the energy crisis results from a physical shortage of energy resources in the world. It advances the alternative case that the crisis is political and economic in nature and that the crisis results in the first instance from the structure of the world oil industry.

That the world faces crisis is beyond dispute. But the crisis flows from the renewal of fierce economic rivalries among the great industrial nations. Above all, the crisis is the result of the desperate efforts

1

of the United States to maintain its international dominance in the face of the rise of Japan and western Europe.

Today, the United States has embarked on the quest for energy self-sufficiency, a new energy strategy that has fundamental implications for the economic and political relations of the western powers.

In particular, the new American energy strategy has vital implications for Canada. Canada has developed as America's northern resource frontier. Its energy resources have been exploited in response to continental rather than Canadian demand. Increasingly in the past two decades, the United States has singled out Canada as a preferred source of resource imports, and has accorded Canadian resources domestic status and exempted them from import quotas.

Today, American policy makers intend to achieve energy self-sufficiency for the United States in part through the inclusion of Canadian resources in the domestic supplies of the United States. Since 1960, Canadian energy policy has evolved in a continental rather than in a Canadian framework. Given the record of the past decade, American policy makers have every reason to feel confident that, in spite of minor obstacles, they can continue to regard Canada as a secure resource base.

For Canada, the energy crisis is a crisis of industrial policy. The launching of a new American energy strategy confronts Canada with a crucial choice, one that will point this nation's economy either in the direction of further continental integration or toward independence.

The threatened breakdown of the world economic system into warring regional blocs could leave Canada in the position of a hinterland in the American bloc. This would not be a happy fate in a period of economic recession or depression when the U.S. will be strongly motivated to export the burdens of its own economic misfortunes to dependent countries under its sway.

Finally, for Canada, the energy crisis is a crisis of Canadian politics. It provides an acute test of the capacity of the Canadian political system to act in defence of the vital interests of the Canadian people.

2   **The World of Oil**

Former U.S. Secretary of the Interior Stewart Udall has been touring the United States preaching the gospel of thrift in energy use. In gloomily lit St. John's Episcopal Church in Youngstown, Ohio, he told the congregation that the energy crisis is a good thing, because it will force a change in human values. He spoke rapturously of the moral benefits of self-denial:

> An end to wastefulness, the practice of thrift, is always good for an individual or a nation. If we have to trim down, slim down, tighten our belts a little more, help each other—who knows? It may be that our society will be a happier, healthier place, and we'll all live richer lives.[1]

The energy crisis has called forth effusive moral statements that signal an attempted return to the ancient values of the American republic. Oil company advertisements now call upon the householder to save energy, and provide helpful hints on how to cut corners on energy use. U.S. President Richard Nixon has solemnly informed the nation that the thermostats have been turned down in every room in the White House.[2]

Learned scholars are proclaiming that the energy crisis has taught us the wickedness of consumption. Above all else, they have told us, we must not encourage the poor in the affluent nations, or the poorer nations as a whole, to aspire to the level of consumption now enjoyed by the few.

In the space of a few years, the energy problem has moved from being a series of short-term supply difficulties to the position of a crisis that appears to threaten the very future of industrial civilization. The crisis is chiefly an oil crisis, since it is access to plentiful supplies of reasonably priced oil that now is the problem.

3

To Canadians the energy crisis appears to be a spillover of the American crisis. But the American energy crisis has itself occurred as part of a dramatic change in the price and availability of oil throughout the capitalist world. The American crisis can only be understood in the wider context of the world energy picture.

Are we living through the first days of a new era of petroleum shortages that signal the beginnings of an energy-scarce society? Or is the energy crisis a human creation, rooted in politics and social structures, rather than in the earth's supply of resources?

Estimating the size of the earth's remaining oil reserves is a perilous venture. Existing estimates are drawn either from sources in the oil industry or from government agencies in various countries. Any estimate of the world's oil reserves must suffer from two serious deficiencies: the possible existence of bias in the source of the estimate (whether from the oil industry or from government), and the sad state of our present knowledge of the earth's resources due to a lack of thorough exploration of most of the planet's surface.

Within these limits, what then is the likely extent of the world's oil reserves?

A 1973 report of the Organization for Economic Cooperation and Development (OECD) placed current world-wide proven reserves of conventional oil at 583.5 billion barrels, or roughly a thirty-two year reserve at present rates of consumption. (The OECD is the economic club of the western powers; it includes the western European countries, Japan, the U.S. and Canada.) The report estimated that the world's ultimate reserves of conventional crude oil, onshore and offshore, are at least four times the size of current proven reserves, or more than 2200 billion barrels. This would amount to reserves good for about 125 years at present rates of consumption. The report goes on to point out that these figures are not estimates of the total reserves of conventional oil, but rather of the portion of conventional oil that is recoverable through current methods of extraction. Since present methods result in the recovery of only 30 per cent of oil from deposits, the amount of conventional crude available could be considerably increased through the evolution of new recovery techniques.[3] The importance of such techniques is evident from the fact that increasing the rate of recovery from 30 to 31 per cent of deposits would in itself add one year to the world's present proven reserves.

In addition to conventional crude oil there are non-conventional sources of crude, such as the world's oil sands and oil shales, which can only be utilized through extraction methods that differ from those used to recover conventional crude. The Canadian government's energy report of June 1973 estimates that the oil sands in Alberta contain 301 billion barrels of ultimately recoverable crude, or roughly half as much as the world's present thirty-two-year reserve of conventional crude.[4] The report then makes the point that Canada's oil sands form only a small proportion of the world's non-conventional oil sources. The report estimates the world's oil sands and oil shales to be about one hundred times as large as the Alberta oil sands.[5] This estimate would mean that these non-conventional sources of recoverable crude oil contain potential reserves fifty times as large as today's proven conventional reserves, or enough for 1500 years in terms of present world consumption.

This estimate is high in relation to other available estimates of the extent of potential non-conventional reserves. The 1973 OECD report placed the extent of oil sands and oil shales as low as six times the present proven conventional reserves, or as little as 190 years' supply at present rates of consumption. The report conjectured that the oil sands and oil shales could be considerably larger than this.[6]

Whatever the extent of oil sands and oil shales, most estimates agree that ultimately the largest supply of oil will come from the conversion of coal to oil. Coal is by far the world's most plentiful fossil fuel. A 1971 issue of *Scientific American* magazine devoted to the energy question estimated that 88 per cent of the energy content available to the world in the form of fossil fuels exists in the form of coal. The report calculated that while world production of conventional oil would likely peak somewhere between the year 1990 and 2000, coal production would peak somewhere in the period 2100 and 2150, with less than 10 per cent of the world's coal reserves exhausted by the year 2000.[7]

The OECD report estimates that the amount of oil ultimately available from coal is larger than the amount available from all other sources combined, or at least 320 years' supply at current rates of production.[8]

Since World War II the world's consumption of energy has been doubling roughly once every ten years. As can be appreciated, this rate of increased energy use, if continued for many more decades, would shrink the world's fossil fuel reserves very quickly indeed. But before such growth in rates of fossil fuel use could continue for many more decades, other limiting factors would come into play, for example, the problem of the disposal of waste heat.

Furthermore, it is highly likely that before many more decades go by, new sources of energy such as various forms of solar energy will increasingly take the burden off the use of fossil fuels by mankind.

The range of estimates presently available to us makes one thing abundantly clear: there is no shortage of oil in the world for the short- to intermediate-range future. The current energy crisis does not represent a sudden transition from an oil-rich to an oil-poor world.

The world's present proven reserves of conventional oil are highly concentrated in one small area of the globe. Over 60 per cent of present world reserves, an estimated 367.4 billion barrels, are concentrated in the countries that ring the Persian Gulf in the Middle East.[9] Between 1965 and 1970 the Middle East increased its share of output from 26.5 to 29.3 per cent of the global total.[10] During the same period the growth in new reserves outside the Middle East was concentrated mainly in Africa, especially in Nigeria and Libya.[11] African production accounted for 12.7 per cent of world output in 1970 compared with 6.8 per cent in 1965. During this same period, the western hemisphere's contribution to world output declined: the U.S. share dropped from 27.8 per cent to 22.8 per cent; Canada remained the same at 2.9 per cent; and other western hemisphere countries (mainly Venezuela) declined from 15.4 to 11.8 per cent.[12]

Although there is plenty of oil in the world for the short- to middle-range future, that oil must make its way to industrial and individual consumers from a relatively small number of producing areas. And oil is extracted and delivered in usable form to consumers by the world's most powerful industry.

The oil industry is dominated by seven gigantic multi-national corporations. Five of these are American: Exxon Corporation, Mobil, Gulf, Texaco, and Standard Oil of California. Two are European: The Royal Dutch/Shell Group, which is British- and Dutch-controlled, and British Petroleum, which is British-controlled.

Exxon Corporation is the giant among the giants. Incorporated in 1882 as the Standard Oil Company of New Jersey, the corporation was built by John D. Rockefeller into a trust that controlled the oil industry on a world-wide basis. In May 1911, the U.S. Supreme Court ruled that the company was a combination in violation of the Sherman Anti-Trust Act. The mighty trust was divided into thirty-three separate companies. But that was not the end of Jersey Standard. The company has since built an empire that under its present name, Exxon, controls assets that make the old Standard Oil trust look small.[13]

Through its dozens of subsidiaries, Exxon operates in more than a hundred countries, including Canada where its subsidiary Imperial Oil is the nation's largest oil company. In 1972, the gross operating income of the multi-national corporation amounted to $20.3 billion, considerably more than the annual revenue of the government of Canada. The corporation's world-wide profit amounted to $1.5 billion, and the undistributed surplus of the corporation stood at $8.9 billion.[14]

Exxon controls reserves of just under fifty billion barrels of crude oil and natural gas liquids, an amount equal to almost 10 per cent of the reserves of the capitalist world. The staggering extent of the corporation's reserves can be illustrated by the fact that they amount to slightly more than the total proven oil reserves of the United States or roughly five times the Canadian proven reserves. Thirty-four billion barrels of Exxon's reserve are located in operations in the Middle East and Africa. In 1972, Exxon's world production of crude oil averaged over six million barrels a day, one-tenth of global production.[15]

It is widely believed that multi-national corporations, like Exxon, serve as a mechanism for providing capital from rich countries like the United States for the development of other parts of the world. An examination of Exxon's financial statements reveals that for it, as indeed for most multi-national corporations, the reverse is true.

The corporation, after a small initial investment abroad, has for a long time financed its foreign operations through their own internally generated profits. If we look at the corporation's annual statement for 1972, we find that over half its profit or $819 million was made *outside* the United States. In that year Exxon paid $851 million in dividends to its shareholders, the overwhelming majority of whom are Americans (the rest of the profit, $680 million, was added to the company's undistributed surplus). Inside the United States the company's profit was $713 million, or almost $140 million less than the dividends paid out to Exxon's American owners. Thus, we can see, about one-sixth of the dividends paid out to the shareholders were financed through foreign operations. Since the dividends paid out to American shareholders exceeded profits made in the U.S., it also follows that any net investments the company made in the U.S. were financed by profits made in its overseas operations. Exxon Corporation is actually an enormous *importer* of development capital into the United States as a result of its world-wide operations.[16]

Exxon's extraordinary dominance is evident from the fact that its gross operating income of $20.3 billion was only a shade less than the combined gross operating income of the next three major oil corporations—Texaco, Gulf and Standard of California—which together grossed $20.6 billion.[17]

The power of the four largest American oil corporations derives from their combined production of 16.7 million barrels a day of crude oil and natural gas liquids.[18] This amounted to over one-quarter of the oil production in the capitalist world.

Since the 1920s the world oil corporations have shared markets and have divided the world into spheres of influence for the exploration of oil. In 1928, for example, through the Achnacarry agreement, the heads of Shell, Anglo-Iranian (now BP) and Jersey Standard (now

Exxon) divided markets on a world scale.[19] The agreement parcelled out producing areas to the three giants and sought the elimination of price competition.

That such agreements come into existence does not imply the elimination of struggle amongst the oil giants. Agreements like the one at Achnacarry are like treaties among states. They are honoured as long as they represent the real balance of power among the forces involved. As new factors come into play—wars, nationalization of assets by some producing countries, changes in the power balance among the countries where the oil companies are based, or the discovery of new reserves—new international agreements are worked out that reflect the changed relations of power among the oil giants. When World War II ended and the U.S. replaced Britain as the dominant power in the Middle East, the U.S. giants encroached on the territory of the British oil corporations, taking the lion's share of postwar reserves and markets. The power of the American oil corporations in the Middle East was guaranteed by the American sixth fleet in the Mediterranean, the unchallenged authority in the area until recently when the Soviet Union established its own military presence there too.

That the world oil picture is by no means to be explained simply in terms of geology and technology can be seen by examining some other effects of political factors upon patterns of oil development and trade. The countries that are today's major oil exporters are the countries in which the major oil companies have successfully combated nationalist movements. If, however, the majors lose the struggle, an oil-rich country may lose its place in world oil trade.

A number of countries are no longer among the ranks of the major exporters of oil because they chose to exercise greater control over their petroleum industries. Most significant in this list is Mexico, which in the 1920s was the world's greatest oil exporting country. Once the industry was nationalized in 1938, Mexican oil was shut out of world markets through the major companies' control of transporting, refining and marketing of oil.[20]

Mexico's decline and fall as an exporter led to the rapid development of Venezuelan reserves. During the forties, Venezuela was the number one exporter of oil in the world, and its industry grew quickly until the accession to office in 1948 of a government committed to nationalization of the foreign-owned oil industry. Development of the oil industry was interrupted for a few months until, with the help of the oil companies, a coup d'état installed the Jiminez dictatorship, which over the next decade oversaw the Venezuelan oil industry's greatest period of growth. When the dictatorship was overthrown and a democratic reform government installed in 1958, Venezuela's oil industry entered a new period of slowdown. While the new government did not carry through its programme to nationalize the foreign-owned oil industry, it did end the parcelling out of new land concessions to the oil companies and steadily sought higher oil royalties. In response the oil companies drastically cut back their capital investment in that country. Venezuela's relative position in the world export picture steadily declined until in 1971, it was surpassed as an exporter by each of three middle eastern countries—Saudi Arabia, Kuwait, and Iran.[21]

Similarly, Iran's rise to its present position as an oil exporter was not an uninterrupted process that occurred smoothly in the years following World War II. In 1951, the government of Mohammed Mossadegh nationalized Iran's oil industry. The major oil companies promptly retaliated by shutting Iranian oil out of world markets. Output in other middle eastern countries was instantly turned up to make up the difference. The irregular situation was "normalized" two years later when a CIA-inspired coup eliminated the Mossadegh regime. The pliant new Iranian government, while retaining formal ownership of the oil industry, handed over its operation to a consortium of the major oil companies.[22]

The case of Russia as an oil exporter is also not without interest. Cheap Russian oil became available as an alternative to American oil for western Europe around the turn of the century. World War I and the Russian Revolution in 1917 ended this early phase in the country's history as a significant oil exporter. Since World War II, Soviet oil exports have been developing once more under the hostile, watchful eye of the U.S. government and the major oil companies.[23]

Against this perennial backdrop of political intervention by the oil companies and by the U.S., vast profits were being made. Oil was becoming *the* critical energy resource in the postwar economic recovery of western Europe and Japan. And as the United States became a large scale importer, world oil trade expanded enormously. This attractive business climate and the rapid discovery of new reserves in many parts of the world led many independent oil corporations to challenge the vaunted positions of the seven majors.

Several types of intruders upset the orderly marketing and pricing arrangements that had been established for the fleecing of humanity. They included U.S. national oil corporations that had hitherto confined their activities to the United States itself. In addition, there were state-run operations in a wide range of countries, as well as the oil export operations of the Soviet Union.[24]

During the 1950s expansion of oil reserves and greater competition had a depressing effect on oil prices. The major oil companies were forced to fight to hold onto their markets and this meant price cuts wherever effective competition had made itself felt. The OECD report on oil, reviewing this period stated:

> The pressure of the newcomers on the crude oil market was matched by the efforts of the established companies to increase or at least to maintain their shares of the petroleum market abroad. The inevitable depression in price levels meant that in some areas the return on invested capital was very low.[25]

Price competition and the glut of oil on the international market combined to lower the price of crude oil in the late fifties and early sixties. By 1970 the price of crude oil in the international market was the same as it had been in 1950. This was in sharp contrast with price increases over the same two decades, years in which the price of most other commodities had doubled.

This decrease in prices did not mean that the oil companies became destitute. Production costs fell during the fifties and sixties and the use of oil increased much more quickly than the use of most other commodities. The companies made up in volume of sales what they lost on depressed prices. Despite these considerable compensations, the oil companies must have looked forward to the day when a sellers' market could be re-established in oil.

Depressed world oil prices meant lower royalties per barrel of oil for producing countries. Under the leadership of Venezuela, the world's major oil-exporting nations formed an organization to look out for their mutual interests, the Organization of Petroleum Exporting Countries (OPEC). Founded in 1960 OPEC's purpose was to take action to halt the falling price of oil on international markets and to arrange the best terms for the producing countries with the giant oil companies. OPEC's membership now includes the major exporting nations in Latin America, Africa and the Middle East. Canada is not a member.[26]

The oil companies and the OPEC countries have both common and contradictory interests. They are united in their desire for high prices for oil because it means a high return for all. For this reason, they have an interest in limiting competition in the oil industry that would lead to price cuts or too quick development of new reserves. Despite these common interests, there are important sources of tension between the oil companies and the OPEC countries. Each side naturally wants the lion's share of the spoils. For this reason, producing countries benefit to some degree from the presence of alternatives to the major companies; they often can make better arrangements, from their point of view, with the independents. In turn, the oil companies have an interest in expanding their reserves outside the OPEC countries as a way of threatening the oil-producing countries with their capacity to move elsewhere if their share of the spoils drops too low.

The relationship of the oil companies to the OPEC countries takes place within the larger context of the relationship of the American state to the oil-producing countries. The OPEC countries are, in the main, highly vulnerable to U.S. economic, political and military intervention in their domestic affairs. For example, the ruling regimes in Saudi Arabia and Kuwait would not survive long without the economic and military support of the U.S. Even more independent regimes are constantly open to the threat of U.S. retaliation. However, the struggle of most of the rulers of OPEC countries is to maximize their position within the American empire, not to secede from it.

It can be concluded that the oil companies and the OPEC countries have a common interest in preventing an oversupply of oil from becoming available in the world. It is also safe to conclude that the oil companies are not in favour of the recent efforts of the OPEC countries to increase their percentage of the take.

The effort of the OPEC countries to improve their position in relation to the oil companies' dates from the organization's sixteenth conference, in June 1968. At this meeting, OPEC members established a set of long-term development objectives concerning their oil industries. These included: a preference for developing the resource through a company based in the producing country; increases in royalties and tax revenues flowing to the producing countries; government determination of the price from which taxes are calculated; the right of the government of the producing country to acquire a participating ownership of the oil industry along with the foreign oil companies.[27]

In subsequent conferences and agreements, the OPEC countries have moved to increase their royalties and taxes and have, in some cases, taken action to acquire a percentage of ownership of the industry.[28]

When governments in producing countries like Saudi Arabia decide to take a piece of the action in their domestic oil industry, they do so through full compensation of the oil industry. What this means is that while the country's oil is being depleted, its government provides the oil companies with additional revenues to explore and develop properties elsewhere. This type of partial government ownership deprives the oil companies of nothing. It actually operates like an extended depletion allowance.

Moreover, partial nationalization of the oil industry gives the oil-producing country an increased stake in the orderly marketing of the product—an added incentive to refrain from political grandstanding. For a nation like Saudi Arabia, with its antique social structure and its monarchy, adventures that harm the oil industry pose equally unwelcome threats internally to the ruling regime. The country's Harvard-educated oil minister, Ahmed Zaki Yamani may well be sincere when he sees the giant oil companies, through their Saudi Arabian consortium Aramco, operating in his country until their lease expires in 1999.[29]

Notes

[1]*Wall Street Journal*, January 28, 1974.

[2]*Congressional Quarterly*, November 17, 1973.

[3]Report of the OECD Oil Committee, *Oil: The Present Situation and Future Prospects* (Paris, Organization for Economic Cooperation and Development, 1973) pp. 51-52.

[4]Canada, Department of Energy, Mines and Resources report, *An Energy Policy for Canada—Phase I* (Ottawa, Department of Energy, Mines and Resources, 1973), v. 1, p. 87.

[5]*Ibid.,* p. 133.

[6]OECD Oil Committee Report, *op. cit.,* p. 52.

[7]*Scientific American,* September 1971.

[8]OECD Oil Committee Report, *op. cit.,* p. 52.

[9]*Ibid.,* p. 55.

[10]*Ibid.,* p. 67.

[11]*Ibid.*

[12]*Ibid.*

[13]*Moody's Industrial Manual* 1973, Moody's Investors' Service, Inc., New York, N.Y., p. 754.

[14]*Ibid.,* pp. 760-761.

[15]*Ibid.,* pp. 757-758.

[16]*Ibid.,* p. 759.

[17]*Ibid.,* pp. 682, 3363, 3408.

[18]*Ibid.,* pp. 681, 758, 3363, 3407.

[19]Robert Engler, *The Politics of Oil* (The University of Chicago Press, 1961) p. 70.

[20]Peter R. Odell, *Oil and World Power* (London, Penguin, 1970) p. 60.

[21]*Ibid.,* p. 65

[22]*Ibid.,* p. 73.

[23]*Ibid.,* p. 43.

[24]*Ibid.*, p. 6.

[25]OECD Oil Committee Report, *op. cit.*, p. 71.

[26]Odell, *op. cit.*, p. 9.

[27]OECD Oil Committee Report, *op. cit.*, p. 80.

[28]*Ibid.*, p. 80.

[29]*Forbes*, February 15, 1973.

3 Profits and National Security: The Old American Oil Strategy

Just as the problem of falling postwar oil prices inspired the formation of OPEC, it was one of the key factors leading to the decision to cut the giant United States market off from those of the rest of the world. A major factor in the postwar oil situation was the rapid decline of U.S. domestic production in relation to world production.

In 1948, the U.S. began to run a deficit in its oil production. In 1950, U.S. domestic production of crude oil totalled 1,874 million barrels, or 52 per cent of the total world production of 3,803 million barrels.[1] By 1970, U.S. crude oil production stood at 3,517 million barrels, which was just over one-fifth of the world production of 16,690 million barrels. In 1970 the U.S. imported 483 million barrels of crude oil and 764 million barrels of refined oil.[2] This amounted to about one-third of the oil used in the United States. The change can be demonstrated by the fact that in 1950 net imports amounted to less than 10 per cent of the oil used in the United States.[3]

Although domestic American production has been losing its dominant world position, the period since World War II has been the era of paramountcy for the American oil corporations. The growing disparity between the declining position of American domestic oil production and the world power of the American oil giants has been a major unsettling factor in the politics of oil since World War II.

Imports into the American market were stepped up by the major oil corporations and the independents that had cashed in on the new low cost reserves in the Middle East and Venezuela. In opposition to these heightened imports was the formidable political lobby of domestic American oildom. The lobby consisted of domestic American oil operations that were not profiting from the importation of cheap foreign crude, and was backed by the millions of Americans whose land is leased to oil companies for exploration (about 25 per cent of the continental United States is regarded as potential petroleum territory). In its alternate guise of the superpatriot wing of the Republican Party, the domestic oil lobby fought imports on the ground that they imperilled American national security.

The drive for profit on the part of every element of the American oil industry (the majors, the national companies, the independent exploration companies and many others), interwove in a complex fashion with the dictates of U.S. national security. The interests of the American state are complementary to, although broader than, the interests of the oil companies. The consistent efforts of U.S. administrations to protect the foreign holdings of U.S. oil companies abroad demonstrates their close community of interest. But the U.S. state also concerns itself with the well-being of other corporate sectors besides that of oil and acts to maintain the world-wide military power of the United States. For this reason, the U.S. state, prodded by the U.S. military, has placed a very high premium, for its own reasons, on the *security* of American oil supplies.

In 1954, the Eisenhower administration established a cabinet-level Advisory Committee on Energy Supplies and Resources Policy to study the security implications of the growing importation of crude oil into the United States. Following the report of the committee, which warned that increased imports of crude oil would constitute a threat to U.S. national security, President Eisenhower asked the American oil companies to limit voluntarily their imports of crude oil into the United States. [4]

The U.S. voluntary import control programme in 1954, revised in 1958, was ineffective in preventing increased imports into the U.S. In 1959 the Eisenhower administration imposed mandatory controls intended to ensure that imports could only increase at a rate equal to the growth of U.S. consumption—about 5 per cent per year (as compared to the 15 per cent annual growth rate for imports during the fifties before mandatory controls). [5]

The preservation of the greater part of the American market for domestically produced crude oil was an act of great international significance, both economically and politically. The continuing competitiveness of highly priced U.S. crude in the American market was protected. U.S. crude, with production costs of $3.00 per barrel could now hold its own in American coastal markets against middle eastern crude that could be produced and shipped to the same markets for less than $1.50 per barrel. This was, of course, good news to American domestic oil producers.

Mandatory controls were also set up in such a way as to guarantee the position of the major oil companies against the interloping independents that had gone abroad in the fifties. Importing rights were vested in corporations termed "traditional" importers.[6] This handed the majors the bulk of import rights under the quota system. Such a system also meant windfall profits for the majors. Since high cost American domestic crude set the overall price for crude in the United States, the majors, with their import rights, could sell foreign oil produced and shipped for half the cost of American crude at the going American price.

Thus, mandatory controls were advantageous for the majors, for the American national petroleum operations, and for the superpatriots who prayed for oil bonanzas on their land.

But American consumers suffered. By the end of the sixties, they were paying five billion dollars a year more for their oil than they would have paid on the open world market.[7] Moreover, mandatory controls, by limiting the access of U.S. consumers to available imports, also had the effect of lowering the price of oil in western Europe and Japan. Thus, the U.S. import policy of the sixties raised U.S. industrial costs and lowered the industrial costs of America's chief capitalist competitors.

Significantly, American attitudes to the various foreign oil-producing states began to be reflected in the import quotas based on national security concerns. In October 1955, the U.S. Office of Defense Mobilization (ODM) exempted Canada and Venezuela from the controls, which were not yet mandatory. Arthur S. Flemming, director of ODM, explained this move later when he stated that "it has always been the policy in Government. . . to consider those countries (Venezuela and Canada) and others in this hemisphere as within the U.S. orbit when dealing with defense questions."[8]

The second Eisenhower voluntary import control programme removed the exemption on Venezuelan and Canadian crude. But this reversal of American policy was soon undone in 1959 when the Eisenhower administration brought in its programme of mandatory controls on crude oil imports. On April 30, 1959, the mandatory programme was amended to exempt "crude oil, unfinished oils, or finished products which are transported into the United States by pipeline, rail, or other means of overland transportation from the country where they were produced, which country, in the case of unfinished oils or finished products, is also the country of production of the crude oil from which they were processed or manufactured."[9]

The exemption, which applied only to Canada, was maintained under presidents Eisenhower, Kennedy and Johnson. Under the mandatory programme, the importing of Canadian crude oil shot ahead. While controls did not prevent the growth of imports relative to

American output during the sixties, they did check it. In 1960 net imports of crude oil and oil products accounted for about 23 per cent of the domestic market compared with 33 per cent 10 years later.[10] Significantly, though, the increase in imports was very largely accounted for through the upswing in Canadian exports to the U.S., since Canada was the only country exempted from the mandatory import controls.

In 1959 Canadian oil accounted for only 8.3 per cent of U.S. imports, while by 1970 Canadian imports stood at over 20 per cent of the total.[11] During this period American imports from Canada quadrupled while imports from other countries only doubled. The proportion of imports to domestic oil only increased from 21 per cent to 26 per cent between 1959 and 1970 if Canadian imports are not included.

Canada's exemption under the mandatory controls did not mean complete access for Canadian crude to the U.S. market, for a number of reasons. First, there was a definite limit imposed by pipeline capacity in moving Canadian oil to the U.S. Second, the import system meant that U.S. producers were granted an import quota based on the amount of domestic crude they used. The use of Canadian crude did not gain them the further import points that would allow them to purchase cheaper middle eastern and Venezuelan oil. Also, a 1967 Canada-U.S. gentleman's agreement not to flood the U.S. market with cheaper Canadian oil was a factor in limiting our exports. However, the quotas on the voluntary agreement were consistently exceeded. Canadian exports of crude reached a high of 800,000 barrels a day in January and February of 1970.[12]

Then came the Shultz report in February 1970. Entitled *The Oil Import Question: A Report on the Relationship of Oil Imports to the National Security,* the report was prepared by the Cabinet Task Force on Oil Import Controls, which was appointed by President Nixon shortly after his administration took office. The task force, chaired by Secretary of Labour George P. Shultz, now secretary of the treasury, was made up of six cabinet members and personnel from a number of American government bureaus. The task force did not achieve a consensus on the matters under its purview. Three of its members (former Secretary of the Interior Walter Hickel, ex-Secretary of Commerce Maurice Stans and Federal Power Commission Chairman John N. Nassikas), submitted a separate report.[13]

The central issue in contention between the main and the separate report was whether the U.S. should adopt a tariff policy for imports of crude oil (the majority position), or retain its import quota system on a modified basis (the minority position). Both groups within the task force agreed on the great importance of a dependable oil supply to

American national security. They disagreed on the degree of the security problem and on how to protect national security (through tariffs or quotas). [14]

The majority position, the use of tariffs, would have opened up wider opportunities for importing foreign crude. The minority position, in effect accepted by default by the administration, advocated the more restrictive continuance of import quotas. Both the majority and the minority groups on the task force were agreed on the efficacy of an energy deal with Canada which would guarantee long-term high volume imports of crude from Canada. [15]

The Shultz report's treatment of Canada's petroleum reserves as a potentially secure addition to American domestic reserves continued a tradition which had been developing over a period of fifteen years.

But the Shultz report was produced just as the energy crisis was beginning to be felt in the United States. U.S. domestic oil production was simply not increasing rapidly enough to maintain the existing ratio of domestically produced to imported oil. While the Shultz report's concern with national security would continue to represent the prevalent attitude of American decision makers, only a new energy strategy for America could realize its objectives.

Notes

[1] U.S. Department of Commerce, Bureau of the Census, *Statistical Abstract of the United States 1972* (Washington, D.C., U.S. Department of Commerce, 1972) p. 658.

[2] *Ibid.*

[3] *Ibid.*

[4] Edward H. Shaffer, *The Oil Import Program of the United States* (New York, Praeger, 1968) p. 109.

[5] Peter R. Odell, *Oil and World Power* (London, Penguin, 1970) p. 30.

[6] *Ibid.*, p. 33.

[7] U.S. Cabinet Task Force on Oil Import Controls report (the Shultz report), *The Oil Import Question, A Report on the Relationship of Oil Imports to the National Security* (Washington, D.C., U.S. Government Printing Office, 1970) p. 22.

[8] Shaffer, *op. cit.*, p. 109.

[9] *Ibid.*, p. 110.

[10] *Statistical Abstract of the United States 1972, loc. cit.*

[11] Canada, Department of Energy, Mines and Resources report, *An Energy Policy for Canada—Phase I* (Ottawa, Department of Energy, Mines and Resources, 1973), v. 2, p. 308.

[12] James Laxer, *The Energy Poker Game* (Toronto, New Press, 1970) p. 29.

[13] *Ibid.*, p. 62.

[14] *Ibid.*, p. 29.

[15] *Ibid.*

4   The Oil Price Revolution of 1973

By 1970, the oil companies and the OPEC countries had begun to turn the corner on the price of oil. The buyer's market of the late fifties and sixties was becoming a seller's market.

The announcement by the Federal Power Commission in 1969 that the United States was beginning to run out of natural gas was the event that ushered in the energy crisis in the United States.[1] In the Middle East the continued closure of the Suez Canal following the Six Day War of 1967, in conjunction with a shortage of oil tanker capacity, led to price increases and supply problems for Europe by the seventies.[2]

These favourable circumstances of looming tight supply were the occasion for OPEC's offensive for higher prices. At the organization's twenty-first conference, held in Caracas, Venezuela in December 1970, the oil-producing nations drew up a list of collective demands for changes in their financial arrangements with the oil companies. In the first half of 1971, the OPEC countries and the oil companies signed new agreements, which increased the percentage of the price of a barrel of oil going to the oil-producing countries in the form of royalties and taxes.[3] Between 1970 and 1973, the posted price of crude oil from the Middle East moved up from about $1.80 a barrel to about $3.00 a barrel.[4]

But 1973 was the year the supply crisis reached proportions that made possible a revolution in the price of oil on a world-wide scale. In the United States, the year began with regional shortages of heating oil; by summertime the shortages were of gasoline. American domestic production was failing to keep up with demand. The American Petroleum Institute (API) announced that U.S. imports of crude oil increased by 31 per cent in the first ten months of 1973 in comparison with imports the year before. And this jump in imports occurred at the same time as U.S. domestic demand increased by only 6.8 per cent.

21

What had happened was an actual *drop* in U.S. domestic oil production.[5]

The American energy crisis was in full swing *before* war in the Middle East helped it along in October 1973.

Why had the energy crisis developed? How could the American petroleum industry, with a century of experience behind it, have failed to respond sufficiently to the upswing in U.S. oil demand? Was the industry faced with physical shortages in American petroleum reserves that were simply beyond its control?

That the problem *did not stem* from a unavoidable shortage of conventional crude oil in the U.S. can be seen from the OECD oil report's estimate that one-half of the crude oil reserves in the U.S. are still waiting to be discovered (let alone non-conventional sources many times larger that have not been developed).[6] During the sixties investment by the oil industry in the U.S. in exploration was so sluggish it fell below the industry's budget for advertising. In addition, the industry allowed a drastic refinery shortage to develop.[7] Detailing the industry's failure to explore, the OECD report stated:

> In the sixties, the rate of capital spending fell below actual needs, particularly in exploration expenditures in the United States where spending rose only by 6.4 per cent for the 11 year period [1960-1971], from $625 million to $665 million, while all other capital expenditures were rising 59 per cent. The results of such a reduced rate of spending show that in 1960 there were 960 barrels of reserves added for each 1,000 barrels of production and had dropped (sic) to only 663 barrels of reserves added for each 1,000 barrels of production in 1969.[8]

The report concluded:

> . . . the potential of oil and gas resources in the United States exceeds by far the performance of the domestic oil and gas industry.[9]

In the United States the shortage of oil was purely a human creation. The oil industry's failure to explore sufficiently for new sources and its failure to establish adequate new refining facilities had led to the crisis. There are two plausible explanations that would account for the oil industry's failure to keep pace with the growth of oil demand: either the industry had, through sheer incompetence, underestimated the demand for oil; or the industry had deliberately planned the shortages.

Naturally, whenever the industry must choose between these two explanations of the crisis, it leans reluctantly to the former. In a speech to the Economic Club of Detroit in January 1974, J.K. Jamieson, chairman and chief executive officer of the Exxon Corporation, explained that the oil industry had underestimated U.S. energy demand for all sources of energy by about 5 per cent:

> We underestimated the pace of economic activity and failed to anticipate the new need for energy to clean up the environment.
> We made an even bigger error in our forecast of oil consumption. This we underestimated by about 10 per cent.[10]

Although the oil industry nobly accepts the blame for having underestimated demand, it claims that the shortages were really created by bungling bureaucrats who insisted on interfering in the functioning of a free enterprise economy. Oilmen like to claim that they are committed to the principle that unhindered market forces can solve problems of supply whenever they occur. Here is the accepted oil industry recipe for solving the problem of shortages:

1. Let oil prices rise to their natural market levels, so that the incentive to explore for new reserves will be maximized;
2. Higher prices will provide a disincentive to individuals and industries to consume energy, thus ending the immediate shortage;
3. The discovery of new reserves will lower costs; and
4. Finally, if a shortage of supply persists, then the free market will provide the best incentive for men to seek substitutes for the commodity that is in short supply.

These axioms of Adam Smith's eighteenth century analysis of capitalism assume, of course, the existence of a very large number of highly competitive small firms in the industry, none of which can effectively corner supply or set prices through its monopoly position. (Hardly the position of a company like Exxon.)

Such homilies are the sum and substance of most current pronouncements by spokesmen on behalf of the American petroleum industry. Even the sophisticated *Wall Street Journal* allows itself such fantasies, as in the case of a long feature article that appeared on the paper's editorial page in November 1973. The article warns against allowing governments to establish regulations that would upset the free functioning of the market. Authored by Dr. W. Philip Gramm, a professor of economics at Texas A and M University and a consultant to Canada's Department of Energy, the article takes the form of a fable about an earlier energy crisis. The moral to the story is: "Mankind has frequently experienced instances of increasing scarcity, and by ingenuity and free action has solved all of them."

Dr. Gramm reminds us that prior to the present petroleum epoch, the major source of fuel for artificial light in the U.S. and Europe was whale and sperm oil. Faced with no alternative source of artificial light and with mushrooming demand, but a scarcity of whales, the world faced an energy crisis. Between 1823 and 1865, Dr. Gramm tells us, the price of sperm oil rose from 43 cents to $1.45 a gallon. Then the price increase got completely out of hand because of difficulties associated with the American Civil War, and in 1866 the price of a gallon of sperm oil rocketed to $2.55.

But, Dr. Gramm coolly tells us—as we sit on the edge of our seats fearing the return of western man to the cave—"economic man" had meanwhile discovered petroleum in Pennsylvania in 1859, and unencumbered by government bureaucrats, he knew what to do with it. According to Dr. Gramm:

> The high prices for whale and sperm oil between 1849 and 1867 provided a growing profit incentive to develop an efficient refining process for crude petroleum and induced the investment required for the production of kerosene. Beginning in 1867, kerosene broke the sperm and whale oil market and prices tumbled. By 1896, sperm oil was cheaper than it had been in any recorded period—40 cents a gallon—but whale oil lamps were no more than relics for succeeding generations.

Then he warns:

> Had government possessed the power and volition to ration whale and sperm oil to hold its price down or to levy a tax on oil to reap the gains from the price rise, the shortages would have been catastrophic and the advent of kerosene and other petroleum products might have been delayed for decades.
>
> The whale oil crisis is a case study of how the free-market system solves a scarcity problem. The end product of this process of discovery and innovation is the Petroleum Age in which we live. We owe the benefits and comforts of the present era to free enterprise and the scarcity of whales.
>
> Though there is no long-term "energy crisis" there is a short-term problem. Economic science teaches that shortages cannot exist in free markets. In free markets prices rise in order to eliminate shortages.
>
> The first step in solving the energy shortage is to allow the free market system to work. *All price ceilings and government controls should be eliminated.* [11]

In an article in *Newsweek* magazine, the celebrated American economist Milton Friedman expressed the same point of view:

> The most effective way to cut consumption and encourage production is simply to let the prices of oil products rise to whatever level it takes to clear the market. The higher prices would give each of the 210 million residents of the United States a direct incentive to economize on oil, to find substitutes for oil, to increase the supply of oil. [12]

Both Gramm and Friedman assume that the oil industry is a competitive one and that its behaviour will conform to the classic pattern of "free enterprise". The assumption that there is competition in the American oil industry is now under searching examination in courtrooms and by government commissions in the United States.

In July 1973 the U.S. Federal Trade Commission (FTC) filed a complaint charging the eight largest oil companies with "a clear preference for avoiding competition through mutual cooperation and the use of exclusionary practices."[13] The FTC report alleged that the anticompetitive practices of the oil companies had resulted in gasoline shortages, higher prices, the closing of large numbers of independent gasoline stations and excess profits to themselves.

The report found a lack of competitive conduct "on all levels in which the integrated firms interrelate." Analysing the behaviour of the eight firms, the FTC report stated: "In fact, their behaviour should properly be characterized as cooperative, rather than competitive, with respect to influencing legislation, bidding for crude leases, establishing the price of crude oil, transporting crude oil (and) marketing gasoline."

In the opinion of the FTC, the major oil firms "have behaved in a similar fashion as would a classical monopolist: they have attempted to increase profits by restricting output."

While not concluding that the fuel shortages have been contrived by the major oil firms, the report said that the firms "have used the shortage as an occasion to debilitate, if not eradicate, the independent marketing sector."[14]

Describing the companies involved, the FTC said they were all vertically integrated firms operating at every level in the oil industry: exploring, producing, transporting and refining crude, and transporting and marketing refined petroleum products. In order of their size, the eight corporations were Exxon Corporation, Texaco Inc., Gulf Oil Corporation, Mobil Oil Corporation, Standard Oil Company of California, Standard Oil Company (Indiana), Shell Oil Corporation and the Atlantic Richfield Company.[15]

The report charges that, at least since 1950, the firms named have worked to control and limit the supply of crude oil available to independent refiners and potential entrants into refining.[16]

A few days after the FTC filed its complaint, a report of the U.S. Federal Power Commission charged that a few firms controlled virtually all the known uncommitted reserves of natural gas in the United States.

The FPC report showed that for the U.S., excluding Alaska, 48.4 per cent of the uncommitted reserves in the country were controlled by the four largest gas-producing companies, and that 67.5 per cent of the reserves were tied up by the eight largest companies. In some key producing areas that account for much of the U.S. total supply of natural gas, the FPC report stated that the large companies controlled 90 to 100 per cent of the reserves.[17]

Even as these reports from two federal government agencies in the U.S. were being issued, the Antitrust and Monopoly subcommittee of the U.S. Senate was investigating the state of competition in the natural gas industry and the reliability of the industry's public estimates of gas reserves.

The Senate investigation was concerned with the controversial issue of whether the price of natural gas in the U.S. should be de-regulated, as the Nixon administration advocates. De-regulation, the Nixon administration asserts, would allow the price to rise to what the market would command, thus providing the incentive for exploration that would wipe out America's natural gas shortage.

Alternatively, the Senate investigators suspect that the gas shortage has been contrived by the producers precisely as a means of ending price controls that presently benefit the consumer.

When FPC Chairman John Nassikas appeared before the Senate subcommittee to present the Nixon administration's view that the shortage of natural gas could be solved if the price was de-regulated, the subcommittee chairman, Senator Philip A. Hart (D. Michigan), challenged the assumption.

Senator Hart charged that along with natural gas reserves being concentrated in a few hands, there is "intermingling and interdependence of producers" because of consortium, joint operating and marketing arrangements, joint bidding and substantial trading of products and tracts of land. He said, "The industry is very much like a family and to allow prices to be set on the premise that free market forces are at work in this industry may ignore reality."[18]

Chairman of the New York State Public Service Commission and former FPC Chairman Joseph C. Swidler testified before the subcommittee that an unregulated market "cannot be counted on to protect residential and other high priority gas consumers" and may lead to excessive prices for natural gas.[19]

In addition to these federal reports and investigations into the lack of competition in the oil and natural gas industries, the State of Florida is taking fifteen major oil companies to court, charging them with conspiracy to create a monopoly that has hindered Florida's ability to purchase gasoline and has driven independent oil dealers out of business.[20]

But the evidence of collusion among the American oil companies should come as no surprise to the Nixon administration. In addition to the long history of marketing and pricing arrangements on a world basis, and of open government-backed cartel arrangements during the 1930s, there is the fact that the Nixon administration in December 1970 itself approved joint action by the oil companies in their negotiations with the OPEC countries. Implied in this were inter-company agreements not to invade one another's markets, especially in western Europe.[21]

At a press conference in January 1974, J.K. Jamieson, chairman and chief executive officer of Exxon, confirmed in a speech that the Nixon administration had exempted the American oil companies from certain antitrust rules so that they could jointly prepare their negotiating positions with Arab governments.[22]

That the oil industry is monopoly-dominated and avoids competition is beyond question. In addition to its failure to live up to the free enterprise mythology surrounding price competition, the oil industry has also failed to develop substitutes for conventional oil to meet increasing consumer demand. Contrary to oil industry fables about free enterprise and progress, it has been the American government, in the face of consistent oil industry opposition, that has been the trailblazer in pursuit of energy substitutes for conventional oil.

For over half a century, the most widely canvassed substitute for conventional oil in the United States has been the oil shales located in Colorado, Utah and Wyoming. The oil shales are locked in a giant fossil lake that is about 16,000 square miles in extent. Six hundred billion barrels of shale oil are estimated to be contained in this vast field, equal in amount to the world's proven reserves of conventional oil.[23]

The United States Bureau of Mines conducted laboratory experiments with shale oil between 1916 and 1925. Until funds for the programme were cut off in 1929, the Bureau operated an experimental oil shale plant, which it had established in 1925. During the 1920s private ventures came into being to attempt to exploit the oil shales. But these failed in the face of technological difficulties, financial weakness and the plentiful existence of conventional crude.

During World War II, fears of potential oil shortages and threats to oil tankers on the high seas led the U.S. Congress to make provision for research on shale oil and on liquification of coal.

Between 1944 and 1955, $88 million was appropriated by Congress for this work. By the end of this period, while considerable difficulties remained, there was general agreement that the mining of shale, its conversion to crude and its refining into gasoline were feasible from a technical standpoint.[24] By the mid-fifties it was estimated that the cost of a gallon of gasoline produced from shale would be 15 cents compared with 12 cents a gallon for gasoline produced from conventional crude.[25] Thus it was reasonable to expect that as technical progress continued and as demand heightened, with consequent increases in the price of conventional crude, that shale oil operations would become an important energy provider.

In an article in *The Nation,* Roscoe Fleming, a columnist for the *Denver Post,* described the oil industry's successful offensive against government research into coal liquification and shale oil:

> When the war emergency had passed, the oil industry, not prepared to brook this potential competition, began a persistent campaign to close down the programme. It succeeded first with the coal-hydrogenization plant in Missouri, which had cost the taxpayers $50 millions; immediately upon coming into office as Secretary of the Interior, Douglas McKay leased the plant for a song to private industry—and *not* for coal hydrogenation.
>
> The oil lobby found the government's oil-shale research project in the cliffs of the Navy's reserve near Rifle, Colorado, harder to strangle. The Bureau of Mines, which operated it, had advanced cheap, huge scale mining to the point where crushed shale could be brought to the retort at less than 50 cents a ton, and had made equally important progress in retorting the shale (as the process of producing the crude oil from the crushed rock is called).
>
> Mr. McKay, a master in the practice of commissioning the coyotes to look after the sheep, asked a committee from the oil industry to advise him what to do with the Rifle enterprise; not unexpectedly, the committee recommended that it be closed down. Mr. McKay wholeheartedly agreed. Congress proved harder to convince, but only slightly so; after all, its leaders in both House and Senate are good and faithful members of what I call the B.O.P., or Bipartisan Oil Party (more powerful in oil matters than the two major parties). The Rifle project was first virtually wrecked through reduced appropriations, necessitating dismissal of most of the research staff. Finally, on June 30 last year [1956], it was formally closed down and put on a standby basis.[26]

Allan Shivers, governor of Texas at the time of the cancellation of the shale oil programme, clothed the attack on shale oil development in the hallowed language of free enterprise:

> The problem in recent years has not been one of finding a substitute for a limited natural resource but rather keeping ambitious bureaus in the Federal Government from subsidizing synthetic replacements before they are needed. Economic history shows that long before the depletion of any resource a dynamic and free people have replaced it with a better substitute.[27]

The oil industry also blocked the development of oil shales through its strong efforts to prevent the extension to the shale industry of the 27.5 per cent depletion allowance so enjoyed by the oil industry as a means of writing off much of its corporate income tax. (The depletion allowance was reduced to 22 per cent in 1969). Oil shale operations enjoyed only a 15 per cent depletion allowance.[28] Here is a case where the oil industry reversed its usual argument that tax breaks are needed if industry is to venture forth into difficult new environments to provide society with its much needed energy resources.

In addition to efforts to derail projects for the liquification of coal and the development of shale oil, the oil industry has warily fought the use of grain alcohol, both as a fuel and as a raw material for use in the chemical industry. Again the oil industry found itself fighting government research projects that were developed during World War II. The use of alcohol as an oil substitute has a long history, particularly in oil-poor Germany where considerable development was made in this field prior to and during World War II. The American oil industry even contributed to these developments through the research-sharing that existed between the I.G. Farben Co. in Germany and Standard Oil of New Jersey.[29]

Despite the prodigious efforts of the oil companies to prevent the development of substitutes for conventional oil, they have prepared themselves for the time when these substitutes will have to be developed. The oil companies have transformed themselves into diversified energy corporations with operations in oil, natural gas, coal, and uranium, and they have availed themselves of leases on oil-shale rich lands in Colorado.

In December 1971, a subcommittee of the House Select Committee on Small Business reported on the oil industry's acquisition of interests in other energy industries. The report documented that between 1963 and 1969 oil companies had taken over coal firms controlling 36 per cent of the U.S. coal market. The committee disclosed that the major oil companies control 84 per cent of U.S. refining capacity, 72 per cent of natural gas production and ownership of reserves, 30 per cent of domestic coal reserves, over 50 per cent of uranium reserves, and 25 per cent of uranium milling capacity.

The subcommittee report concluded that the growing fuel market concentration "may result in the dwindling of available fuel supplies, the maintenance of artificially high price levels and the eventual reduction in the number of competitors through merger, acquisition or bankruptcy."[30]

In January 1974, the U.S. Department of the Interior began leasing public lands in Colorado to the oil companies to begin shale oil pilot projects.[31] In the House of Representatives, Rep. Charles A. Vanik (D. Ohio) said that the move was a giveaway to "Big Oil". He charged that the oil industry "has deliberately limited their commercial involvement to ongoing studies and research that allow them to keep track of the trends in the industry while waiting for prices to reach profit levels they want."[32]

The record of the American petroleum industry is a clear one: the major oil corporations have cooperated to eliminate price competition and have acted to drive independent producers to the wall; the industry has also worked for decades to avoid a glut of non-conventional energy products which could depress prices.

In the fall of 1973, the efforts of the oil companies to create a sellers' market coincided with the similar efforts of the OPEC countries. The result was the price revolution that followed that Middle East war.

Supposedly in a determined effort to use their oil power to aid the Arab cause against Israel, the major Arab oil-producing states announced that they were cutting back their production of oil by an initial 25 per cent, to be followed by an additional five per cent a month until Israel retreated from the lands it had occupied since the Six Day War of 1967. They further announced a total boycott on oil sales to countries that were pro-Israel: the United States and the Netherlands.[33]

The boycott had peculiar features from the beginning. Although ostensibly aimed at the United States, it had much more devastating implications for Japan and western Europe. Japan is dependent on imports for 99.5 per cent of its oil, and of these imports 85 per cent comes from the Middle East.[34] Western Europe is dependent on imports for over 96 per cent of its oil, over 80 per cent of which comes from North Africa and the Middle East.[35] Apart from non-Arab Iran, the oil-producing states in the Middle East and North Africa took part in the boycott.

The United States is much less dependent on Arab oil than are Japan and western Europe. Not only does U.S. domestic production account for two-thirds of American oil needs, but American dependence on imports from outside the western hemisphere is small indeed. Less than 20 per cent of U.S. oil imports comes from sources in the eastern hemisphere. And of this amount less than half comes from middle eastern countries, including non-Arab Iran. Arab oil accounts for less than five per cent of American supply, far less than that supplied by Venezuela or Canada.[36]

It soon became evident that the Arab boycott was not only oddly directed, but that it involved a very high ratio of rhetoric to actual embargo.

In early December 1973, when the Arab countries were supposed to have cut back production by 20 per cent, the tonnage of tankers sailing from Ras Tanura in Saudi Arabia, the largest Arab terminal, was up 39 per cent over tonnage in December 1972. Tonnage of tankers leaving Kuwait and Iraq was up 39 and 43 per cent respectively. Ironically, the increase in tanker tonnage sailing from non-Arab Iran, a country not involved in any boycott, was only 23 per cent. These tonnage increases over December 1972 were much greater than were the increases in oil consumption in western countries over the one year period.[37]

The British magazine, the *Economist,* reported the presence of large numbers of super-tankers off the British coast, operating as floating stores of oil. The report stated that the oil companies were paying some service station owners to keep their tanks full. These manoeuvres were aimed at holding onto oil cargoes until expected price increases materialized, raising the value of the supply on hand. The oil companies would then realize speculative gains.

The *Economist,* questioning the extent of the Arab boycott, offered the following explanation:

... the Arabs may not have cut production by anything like the amount that they say.

If this is so, there is some logic to explain it. The Arab oil-producers have certainly milked the situation for the maximum political capital, without so far doing anything drastic to destroy the western economies on whose prosperity the value of their dollars depends. The oil firms may have their own reasons for going along with this. ... One could be that they are prepared to help the Arabs save face if it keeps the oil flowing. Another is that they have been warning for some time that there would be an oil shortage, and these warnings have been falling on deaf ears. Many in the industry believe that this winter would have seen an oil shortage anyway, even without the Middle East crisis. The present situation puts all the blame firmly on the Arabs, and increases oil prices.

Higher prices are necessary to generate investment in finding new sources of oil.

It would be wise for western governments to play along with any deception that saved the sensible Arab governments from getting boxed into a position in which they might have to put their threats into action.[38]

Further evidence of the deceptive nature of the boycott came in February 1974, with the Shah of Iran's claim that the United States was continuing to import at least as much oil during the boycott as it had in September 1973. Appearing in New York on a television show, the Shah dismissed the boycott in his remarks to his American audience.

"Why should you care about that [the boycott]? You are not short of oil," he said.

He then asserted that the U.S. had been importing "more oil than at any time in the past."

When asked if the imports of oil in the U.S. were greater in the winter months of 1974 than they had been in September 1973, he replied: "I can't say for sure. But what is certain is that you are not importing less."[39]

The Shah stated that once oil was shipped on tankers from producing countries, its destination was often altered by the oil companies. He concluded that the shortages were being deliberately fostered by the oil companies to increase their profits.

U.S. government officials, of course, continued to claim that the United States was plagued by very real shortages. Federal energy chief William Simon put the amount of the shortfall on gasoline at 15 per cent in February 1974.

Information on which to base firm conclusions on the extent of the shortages caused by the boycott in the United States and the other industrialized nations remains sketchy. The available evidence suggests that the boycott, while far from fully effective, restricted oil supply to a limited degree, before it was lifted in March 1974.

While estimating the extent of the shortfall caused by the boycott is difficult, it is clear that the long efforts of the oil companies to create a sellers' market were greatly assisted by the political atmosphere caused by the Middle East War and its aftermath.

In late December 1973, the OPEC countries raised the price of crude oil from an average of three dollars a barrel to a price ranging from eleven to twenty dollars a barrel.[40] These price hikes actually involved increases in what is called the *tax reference* price of oil. (The tax reference price is the price used by the government of a producing state to determine the level of royalties and taxes payable to it.) The actual selling price of oil to consuming countries depends on the increase the oil companies are able to command over and above the amount of taxes they pay.

It soon became clear that the supply crisis of 1973 meant unprecedented good fortune for the oil companies as well as for the OPEC countries. A *Wall Street Journal* article trumpeted the good news:

The energy "crisis"—the very real shortage of fuel plaguing customers large and small—may be the best thing that's happened to the oil and gas business in a long time.

Responsible for this recent good fortune is a high demand, short-supply situation that seems certain to tighten even further.[41]

The extent of the good news became evident in January 1974 when the oil industry's spectacular year-end profit gains for 1973 were made public.

Exxon Corporation announced that its 1973 profits were up 59 per cent over 1972 to $2.44 billion. That the price increases and boycott undertaken by Arab countries had not hurt Exxon was made evident from the company's announcement that while its U.S. petroleum earnings were up only 16 per cent over 1972, its earnings on eastern hemisphere operations had risen a staggering 83 per cent.

Exxon Chairman J.K. Jamieson justified the huge profit increases as being necessary to cover the company's quickly expanding capital expenditures. He announced that Exxon's 1973 world-wide capital expenditures had risen 12 per cent over 1972 to $2.9 billion. Exxon's projected capital budget for 1974 was placed at $3.7 billion. [42]

Texaco and Mobil both announced giant profit increases for the fourth quarter of 1973. Texaco's profits were up 70 per cent over the fourth quarter of 1972 and Mobil's were up 68 per cent. [43]

The oil price revolution of 1973 was the outcome of the long efforts of the major oil companies to replace a buyers' with a sellers' market in oil. The oil companies had cooperated to eliminate price competition; they had pursued a sluggish pace of exploration for new reserves; and they had suppressed the development of substitutes for conventional oil. The Middle East crisis of 1973 simply speeded up a process already underway.

The result of the oil price revolution was a sudden change in the price of oil in relation in the price of other commodities. The success of the oil companies resulted not simply in a higher price for oil, but, as we shall see in the next chapter, in a readjustment of power relations among the great industrial nations.

For the oil companies, higher profits provided the capital for gigantic new investments. New investments assured huge future profits. Operating as powerful private governments, the oil companies were making decisions that would determine the priorities of the world's major industrial societies.

Notes

[1]James Laxer, *The Energy Poker Game* (Toronto, New Press, 1970) p. 3.

[2]Report of the OECD Oil Committee, *Oil: The Present Situation and Future Prospects* (Paris, Organization for Economic Cooperation and Development, 1973) pp. 71-72.

[3]*Ibid.,* p. 80.

[4]*Ibid.,* pp. 85-89.

[5]*Wall Street Journal,* November 13, 1973.

[6]OECD Oil Committee Report, *op. cit.,* p. 63.

[7]*Ibid.,* p. 94.

[8]*Ibid.,* p. 156.

[9]*Ibid.,* p. 63.

[10]*Globe and Mail,* January 29, 1974.

[11]*Wall Street Journal,* November 17, 1973.

[12]*Newsweek,* November 19, 1973.

[13]*Congressional Quarterly,* July 14, 1973.

[14]*Ibid.*

[15]*Ibid.*

[16]*Wall Street Journal,* July 18, 1973.

[17]*Wall Street Journal,* June 27, 1973.

[18]*Ibid.*

[19]*Ibid.*

[20]*Ibid.*

[21]Peter R. Odell, *Oil and World Power* (London, Penguin, 1970) p. 14.

[22]*Wall Street Journal,* January 29, 1974.

[23]Roscoe Fleming, *The Nation,* March 15, 1965.

[24]Robert Engler, *The Politics of Oil* (The University of Chicago Press, 1961) p. 96.

[25]*Ibid.*

[26]Roscoe Fleming, *The Nation,* May 18, 1957.

[27]Engler, *op. cit.,* p. 98.

[28]*Ibid.*

[29]*Ibid.,* pp. 100-105.

[30]Congressional Quarterly, *Energy Crisis in America* (Washington, D.C., Congressional Quarterly, Inc., 1973) p. 38.

[31]*Denver Post,* November 28, 1973.

[32]*Denver Post,* November 8, 1973.

[33]*The Economist,* December 15, 1973.

[34]OECD Oil Committee Report, *op. cit.,* pp. 46, 64.

[35]*Ibid.,* p. 59.

[36]*Energy Crisis in America, op. cit.,* p. 12.

[37]*The Economist,* December 15, 1973.

[38]*Ibid.*

[39]*Globe and Mail,* February 25, 1974.

[40]*Globe and Mail,* December 26, 1973.

[41]*Wall Street Journal,* August 14, 1973.

[42]*Wall Street Journal,* January 24, 1974.

[43]*Wall Street Journal,* January 25, 1974.

5 Profits and National Security: The New American Oil Strategy

Many of us have heard the adage that the last letters of the word, "American", say "I can." I am confident that we can, and will, meet our national resource challenges.

Richard Nixon
The White House
February 15, 1973

Since 1970, the United States has been approaching a basic national decision on the future of its petroleum industry. Two alternative courses have appeared possible: the importation of increasingly massive amounts of overseas crude oil so that imports would account for two-thirds of U.S. crude by the early 1980s; or the renewed development of both conventional and non-conventional reserves on this continent.

The first choice would lead to multi-billion-dollar energy trade deficits for the U.S. (even at pre-1973 world oil prices). To avoid an impossible balance of payments deficit in this case, the United States would have to increase its export of manufactured goods on a truly mammoth scale. The difficulty with this is that the oil-producing nations of the Middle East have real limitations as potential importers of manufactured goods. They have small populations with a vast disparity of income between a small ruling elite and the rest of the population. At present, the U.S. mainly exports armaments to these nations, but it is highly improbable that these sales could reach an annual level high enough to come anywhere near the point needed to balance the projected U.S. oil deficits.

And if the U.S. could not sell back manufactured goods to the oil-producing nations at the same rate as it bought oil, the oil-exporting countries would have nothing to do with their U.S. dollars

37

except invest them on Wall Street. In addition to being concerned that reliance on imports for two-thirds of U.S. oil would undermine American military security, U.S. decision-makers fear the possibility of significant takeovers of their industries through investments from the oil-producing nations. Also, to make possible the importation of two-thirds of U.S. oil by the early 1980s, a mammoth programme of giant tanker construction and the preparation of North American super-tanker ports would have to begin immediately.

The alternative choice, the quest for U.S. energy self-sufficiency, can only be realized through massive investment in and rapid development of North American conventional and non-conventional petroleum resources.

The evidence is clear that the United States is opting for energy self-sufficiency. In September 1973, President Nixon told newsmen that with respect to oil the U.S. "must develop the capacity so that no other nation in the world that might, for some reason or another, take an unfriendly attitude toward the United States [can have] us frankly in a position where they can cut off our energy."[1]

Once the Middle East War had occurred and the subsequent Arab oil boycott had been announced, the Nixon administration proclaimed what it called "Project Independence", the quest for U.S. energy self-sufficiency by 1980. In a national television address on November 7, 1973, Nixon explained the need for American energy self-sufficiency:

> Today the challenge is to gain the strength that we had earlier in this century, the strength of self-sufficiency. Our ability to meet our own energy needs is directly linked to our continued ability to act decisively and independently at home and abroad in the service of peace, not only for America, but for all nations in the world.[2]

Even before the Middle East War began, the breakdown of the old American energy strategy was apparent. The system of mandatory import quotas on oil was no longer viable because of burgeoning U.S. demand for foreign petroleum due to failing U.S. domestic production.

On April 21, 1973, President Nixon formally scrapped the old Eisenhower import system that had been in operation since 1959. In an energy message to Congress, he stated:

> The current Mandatory Oil Import Program is of virtually no benefit any longer. Instead, it has the very real potential of aggravating our supply problems, and it denies us the flexibility we need to deal quickly and efficiently with our import requirements.
>   Effective today, I am removing by proclamation all existing

tariffs on imported crude oil and products. Holders of import-licenses will be able to import petroleum duty free. This action will help hold down the cost of energy to the American consumer.

Effective today, I am also suspending direct control over the quantity of crude oil and refined products which can be imported. In place of these controls, I am substituting a license-fee quota system.

Under the new system, present holders of import licenses may import petroleum exempt from fees up to the level of their 1973 quota allocations. For imports in excess of the 1973 level, a fee must be paid by the importer.

This system should achieve several objectives.

It should help to meet our immediate energy needs by encouraging importation of foreign oil at the lowest cost to consumers, while also providing incentives for exploration and development of our domestic resources to meet our long-term needs. There will be little paid in fees this year, although all exemptions from fees will be phased out over several years. By gradually increasing fees over the next two and one-half years to a maximum level of one-half cent per gallon for crude oil and one and one-half cents per gallon for all refined products, we should continue to meet our energy needs while encouraging industry to increase its domestic production.[3]

In the short term the U.S. had to face the necessity of increased imports. For the intermediate- and long-range future though, it intended to move toward self-sufficiency. America's emerging energy strategy is based on the following elements and timetable:

Effective immediately:
- A programme to prepare deepwater ports in the U.S. (to facilitate increased crude oil imports).
- Higher oil prices and the de-control of the price of uncommitted natural gas reserves.
- Stepped-up coal output (to enable a reduction in the amount of oil used in the production of electric power).
- Relaxation of environmental standards that now block much expanded strip mining of coal, frown on the use of coal to replace oil in the production of electric power, and delay the bringing on line of new nuclear power plants.
- A concerted programme to build new refineries in the United States.
- Visible symbolic measures like temperature controls in government buildings, bans on ornamental lighting, curtailed limousine service for government bureaucrats and year 'round daylight saving time to prepare Americans psychologically for the higher energy costs they will have to pay.

Effective by the late 1970s:
- Massive efforts to develop commercially viable liquification of

coal and production of shale oil.
- Speeding up the approval and construction of new nuclear power plants.
- Stepped-up production of oil in offshore areas adjacent to the United States.
- Building of the trans-Alaska pipeline system to bring two million barrels of crude oil daily to the continental U.S.
- Large scale increases in natural gas and oil imports from Canada based on gas reserves in the Canadian Arctic and oil in the Alberta oil sands.

Effective by the late 1980s:
- Perfection of the fast breeder nuclear reactor for the production of electric power.
- The harnessing of solar energy.

During 1973, important steps were taken to implement America's new energy strategy.

April 1973: President Nixon announced that he was proposing legislation for federal licensing of offshore deepwater ports beyond the three-mile limit. This was a necessary step to meet the need for short-term increases in the amount of crude oil imported. The announcement came on the same occasion that mandatory oil import quotas were eliminated.

April 1973: Nixon proposed the ending of price regulations for natural gas from new gas wells.[4]

On this occasion Nixon also directed the Secretary of the Interior to triple the annual acreage leased on the outer Continental Shelf by 1979. He estimated that by 1985 these offshore oil reserves could provide for 16 per cent of American oil needs.[5]

July 1973: Nixon pledged ten billion dollars for a federal energy research and development effort over a five-year period to begin in fiscal year 1975.[6]

July 1973: Speedy Congressional approval was granted for the building of the trans-Alaska pipeline system, expected to deliver two million barrels of crude oil per day to the U.S. west coast when completed. The Nixon administration had blasted its way past the objections of environmentalists and succeeded in getting Congress to declare the trans-Alaska project environmentally acceptable (thus overcoming a setback caused when the Supreme Court upheld a lower court ban on construction of the pipeline). By passing legislation that stated that the terms of the U.S. 1969 Environmental Standards Act had been met, Congress prevented any further litigation on the environmental aspects of the pipeline.

The mood in the U.S. was reflected in a statement by Alaska Republican Senator Ted Stevens, justifying the Senate's blocking of the courts: "There is no way to start a pipeline without stopping all the litigation of the environmental extremists."[7]

November 1973: In a national television address Nixon announced measures to prevent industries and utilities that use coal from converting to oil. In addition, efforts were to be made to convert power plants using oil to coal.[8]

On the same occasion, Nixon announced he was asking the Atomic Energy Commission (AEC) to speed up the licensing and construction of new nuclear plants, to cut the time for bringing these plants on line from ten to six years.[9]

It should be pointed out that nuclear scientists not employed by the AEC are enormously concerned about the dangers involved in the American nuclear power programme. Some months prior to the Nixon speech, nuclear physicist Henry W. Kendall, speaking on behalf of the Union of Concerned Scientists, warned that "the central problem with the present nuclear reactor programme is that the pace of construction . . . has far outstripped the pace at which safety technology has been developed."

"The potential hazards are just too large to justify anything less than the greatest care and prudence,"[10] Kendall noted.

Nixon also stated in his November energy crisis address that he intended to present an emergency energy act to Congress, which would provide him with enormous powers to allocate the energy supplies of planes and ships. The act would also provide the authority for relaxation of environmental regulations on a temporary case-by-case basis.[11]

Nixon concluded this address by declaring "Project Independence", the goal of national self-sufficiency in energy by 1980.

Many Nixon pronouncements during 1973 made it clear that self-sufficiency involved large-scale developments in the liquification of coal and the development of shale oil.[12] On one occasion he stated:

> We have half of the coal in the world, and yet we have conversions from coal to oil. Why? Because coal is not a clean fuel. Coal can be made a clean fuel. . . . We have got to get that coal out of the ground and we have to develop the shale oil, for example, which exists in Colorado and some of our western states. That will solve part of the problem.[13]

And in another address, Nixon pointed to the fact that 91 per cent of the hydrocarbons in the ground in the United States exist in the form of coal.[14]

"Project Independence" also depends on another Nixon long-range energy favourite—the fast breeder nuclear reactor. The fast breeder reactor is designed to create as much fissionable material as it uses to generate heat. It would, therefore, solve problems of declining fissionable ore reserves like uranium. The first large-scale breeder reactor is scheduled to be completed by 1980.[15]

November 19, 1973: The U.S. Senate passed a National Energy Emergency Act giving unprecedented peacetime powers to the President to deal with fuel shortages.

The new American energy strategy, involving the intensive development of North American conventional and non-conventional petroleum, means permanently higher energy costs for American industry and individual American consumers. The Canadian government's June 1973 energy report estimated that it will take a price of six dollars a barrel (in constant 1972 dollars), to make U.S. non-conventional reserves, such as the oil shales and liquified coal, economically viable.[16]

This doubling of the price of energy in relation to other commodity prices will significantly affect the living standards of Americans. Not only will consumers pay much more for gasoline, heating oil and electricity, but industrial costs and the costs of food production will be increased. The new American energy strategy will result in a massive redistribution of income from society at large to the oil companies.

The international oil price revolution of 1973 in the aftermath of the Middle East War is the event that has made American self-sufficiency in energy economically feasible. World oil prices have now reached the level where the U.S. can afford to develop the conventional, non-conventional and offshore reserves of North America. To have doubled the price of energy in the United States while leaving the rest of the world paying lower prices would have resulted in industrial costs for the U.S. that would have been higher than those of other countries. It would have priced American manufactured goods right out of world markets.

The new American energy strategy has been conceived in the context of fierce U.S. trade rivalries with Japan and western Europe. The energy strategy is the most important extension of American economic policy since Nixon's economic initiatives in August 1971.

Nixon's economic measures in August 1971 and the new American energy strategy have both been responses to the invasion of the U.S. market by manufactured goods from Japan and western Europe, and the weakening position of American exports since the mid-1960s.

This U.S. industrial weakness, reinforced by the Vietnam War, led to the dollar crisis of 1971 and 1972, which threatened the position of the United States dollar as the reserve currency of the capitalist world. In August 1971, U.S. President Nixon was forced to respond to the challenge to American economic supremacy. The world was startled when Nixon announced that he was taking the U.S. off the gold standard; that he was imposing a 10 per cent surcharge on imports into the United States; that he was seeking upward revaluation of the currencies of America's chief competitors; and that he was proposing incentives for American domestic manufacturing in the form of the 7 per cent investment tax credit for capital investment at home and the Domestic International Sales Corporation (DISC), designed to entice U.S. multi-national corporations to export more from the U.S. while manufacturing less in their branch plants abroad.[17]

The new American energy strategy capitalizes on the control of the bulk of petroleum production in the OPEC countries by the major American oil companies and the dependence of the governments in the OPEC countries on U.S. economic, political and military power. The American state, the American oil companies, and the governments of the OPEC countries have a mutual interest in bringing about a permanent increase in the world price of oil in relation to other commodities. An increase directly benefits the oil companies and the OPEC countries by guaranteeing them a higher return on the sale of oil. The U.S. government supports such an increase both because it profits the oil companies, with their enormous political influence in the United States, and because it makes the programme of American energy self-sufficiency economically viable.

Implied in such an alliance is a changed U.S. role in the Middle East. Kissinger's airport-to-airport diplomacy is precisely aimed at realizing such a new American posture. Three diplomatic moves are involved: Israel must be convinced to pull back from her untenable frontiers won in the Six Day War; special arrangements made with the Arab states, designed to preserve the antique social structures of the oil sheikdoms; and Arab revolutionary nationalism prevented from threatening the artificial boundaries of the area and challenging the power of the oil companies.

A working arrangement between the American state, the oil companies and the governments of the OPEC countries depends further on their mutual ability to force western Europe and Japan to pay much higher oil prices. How good are their prospects for achieving this?

Western Europe will be highly dependent on imports from the OPEC countries, particularly the Middle East producers, until at least the end of the seventies. There are, however, factors which offset European dependence on imported oil. Despite the rise of oil, coal has remained an important energy source in Britain, West Germany and

France. Moreover, enormous new reserves of natural gas in the Netherlands and the North Sea, available at comparatively low costs, have made natural gas an attractive substitute for oil, which will cut into the growth of oil use. Furthermore, oil discoveries in the North Sea may provide western Europe with 15 per cent of its needs by 1980. Western Europe also has the option of importing Soviet oil on a significant scale. Soviet oil has already been penetrating the markets of Italy and Scandinavia to an important extent, and at prices lower than those charged by the majors.[18]

Japan appears to be even more vulnerable, over the middle range, to economic damage caused by much higher oil prices than is western Europe. The Japanese economy is more oil-based than any other industrial country's. Japan's indigenous coal industry has declined to a level that makes it less important than coal in western Europe. Furthermore, although exploration is underway, Japan has not found indigenous land-based or offshore supplies of natural gas on anything like the scale of discoveries in western Europe. Alternative oil supplies, not controlled by the majors, are being sought to some extent. Japanese government-sponsored oil explorations in Japan, in other parts of Asia and in the Middle East promise some relief from the price gouging and control over supply exercised by the major oil companies. Soviet oil is also becoming an alternative to some degree. But, at present, 80 per cent of Japan's oil comes from the Middle East and, except for that provided by non-Arab Iran, was affected by the Arab countries' boycott in the fall of 1973.[19]

To ensure that western Europe and Japan continue to pay the higher oil prices, the U.S. government has intervened in support of the oil companies. In February 1974, the U.S. summoned its major trading partners—the western European nations, Japan and Canada—to Washington for a conference on oil. At the conference U.S. Secretary of State Henry Kissinger sought the creation of a bloc of energy-consuming nations that would operate under American leadership. Formation of such a bloc would ensure the continued dominance of world oil distribution by American companies. Kissinger revealed the basic American support for the new world price when he said at the conference that while oil prices should not get out of hand they would have to remain much higher than they had been before October 1973.[20] (In the winter months of 1974, most observers predicted that with the lifting of the Arab oil boycott, the international price of oil would stabilize at about eight dollars a barrel.)

The purpose of the Washington conference was to prevent bilateral arrangements between America's trading rivals and the producing countries that would bypass the monopoly of the American oil companies. France was the only nation at the conference to challenge the United States directly. France refused to go along with key sections of the communique issued at the end of the conference, which frowned on bilateral arrangements between oil-consuming and oil-producing nations. Instead of following the American course, France made special deals directly with Saudi Arabia and with Libya for long-term oil purchases in return for French assistance in furthering industrial development in those nations.[21]

French bilateralism threatens the new American energy strategy. Other trading rivals of the United States can be expected to follow the French lead to some degree. But, so far, the Americans have had the upper hand in protecting their monopoly position in the world oil industry.

The success of U.S. economic policies, especially those that capitalize on the vulnerability of western Europe and Japan to higher oil prices, is already evident. Even before the Middle East War and the oil price revolution of December 1973, the American trade balance was improving dramatically. In the second quarter of 1973 the U.S. enjoyed a $356 million *surplus* in its official reserve balance, compared with a $4.52 billion *deficit* for the same quarter in 1972.

The quarterly surplus was the first recorded for the United States in three and a half years. The third quarter saw an even more dramatic improvement for the U.S.—a $2.15 billion surplus in the official reserve balance, the highest surplus recorded for the "official reserve transactions" balance since 1960, when statistics for this account were begun.[22]

The improved American payments position pointed to the success of the dollar devaluations and the other Nixon measures in improving America's international position. The oil boycotts and the subsequent announcements in December 1973 by the Arab countries of price increases to eleven dollars a barrel for crude oil weakened the western European and Japanese currencies in relation to the American dollar. If hard times lay ahead for everyone because of energy shortages and price increases, the United States could nonetheless look forward to important gains on its industrial competitors during the coming economic slump.

Not only did the oil price revolution improve America's trade position vis a vis its industrial competitors, it guaranteed that America's competitors would themselves pay for the new U.S. energy strategy. As we saw in the previous chapter, Exxon's spectacular 59 per cent profit increase in 1973 over 1972, came mainly from an 83 per cent increase in its earnings on eastern hemisphere operations (compared with only a 16 per cent increase on its U.S. operations). Since the

U.S. purchases only small amounts of eastern hemisphere oil, Exxon's profits were clearly made at the expense of the Japanese and western Europeans, the chief purchasers of Exxon's eastern hemisphere oil. Higher profits will continue to be necessary on American oil company sales of eastern hemisphere oil if the gigantic sums needed to develop North America's non-conventional reserves are to be realized. During the seventies, capital investments by the oil industry worldwide may reach $550 billion compared with $157 billion during the sixties.[23]

While America's new energy strategy is conceived by the American state as an instrument of competition against foreign rivals, the drive of the oil corporations to double the price of oil in relation to everything else also threatens the power of other sections of American capitalism. Even though American auto, chemical and steel companies will benefit internationally from the far worse fate of western European and Japanese industrialists, they are nonetheless scrambling to protect their power within *American* capitalism.

A *Wall Street Journal* article in January 1974 reports that American industrial giants "have begun an end-run designed to give them favored positions in the competition for natural resources." In order to circumvent oil and natural gas shortages and to avoid paying steep price increases, the companies are plunging into the oil business themselves. Some companies like Bethlehem Steel Corporation and Du Pont Company have formed partnerships with exploration and production companies. Through this means, they get actual ownership of, or first call on, the oil and gas reserves discovered by the outfits they are financing.

Other industrial giants such as General Motors, Ford and Dow Chemical are actually exploring for petroleum on their own land to ensure themselves cheap fuel and raw materials.

The *Journal* report quotes the president of one company as saying that the present "competition [for ownership interests] is so fierce you wouldn't believe it."

Even if the U.S. government decides to ration American petroleum products, the industrial corporations will benefit from the profits made on their petroleum investments and will thus be able to offset the increase in the prices they pay for their own fuel.

The *Journal* article detailed natural gas ventures by Ford and GM in Ohio:

In December [1973] the Ohio Public Utilities Commission approved an agreement between Ford and Columbia Gas of Ohio Inc., under which Ford will develop a natural gas field on property in Morgan County, selling the gas to Columbia. In return, Columbia agreed to pipe 50 per cent of Ford's natural gas to the auto maker's truck plant in Avon Lake, Ohio.

General Motors is petitioning the Ohio commission for permission to enter into a similar deal with East Ohio Gas Co. GM would make 30 per cent to 50 per cent of the natural gas produced from wells on its Lordstown property available to the public utility. In return, Ohio Gas would ship the balance to GM's central foundry in Defiance, a facility sorely strapped for fuel supplies.

The offices of Houston oilmen are being invaded by industrialists interested in joint ventures. As a result, industrial corporations may end up providing the chief financial backing for the ventures of independent petroleum operators.[24] In the present situation, American industrial corporations have a stake in preventing the oil giants from completely massacring the independent oil companies.

The oil industry's spectacular profit gains and the struggle of the manufacturing giants to stave off higher prices for themselves, has sparked U.S. congressional action to hit the oil companies with tax increases. The most serious threat to the industry came from the legislative plans of Democratic Senator Henry Jackson from the state of Washington. The Jackson plan would require that more information be made public about the operations of the oil industry, that the public be represented on the boards of oil concerns, and that major acquisitions, diversifications or market changes receive public clearance.

The Nixon administration itself was proposing changes in the taxing of oil companies: the elimination of the 22 per cent depletion allowance on the foreign exploration activities of the oil companies (with retention of the depletion allowance at home); the ending of the practice of deducting the industry's foreign tax bills directly from the amount owing in American corporate tax—instead foreign taxes would be deducted as an expense; and a windfall tax on crude oil selling for more than $4.75 a barrel, graduated to start at 10 per cent of the increase and sliding upwards to 85 per cent of the increase.

But despite the clamour for action to clip the wings of the oil companies, Washington political insiders did not predict a drastically changed tax climate for the oil industry. Many believed that the Nixon programme would have little effect on the oil industry, since tax write-off options are now so generous that they can't use them all anyway. The Nixon programme was seen as the move of an administration with close links to the oil industry, whose real objective was to prevent serious action by proceeding with its own minor reform proposals. As Charles E. Walker, described by the *Wall Street Journal* as Washington's top business lobbyist, said, "When it all shakes out, I think we'll see a lot of rhetoric and some action but not that much in terms of radical change affecting the industry."

Referring to the chairmen of the tax-proposing House Ways and Means Committee and the Senate Finance Committee, one congressman put it this way, "You don't really think Wilbur Mills and Russell Long are going to castrate the oil industry, do you?"[25]

But just to be sure that there is no damage done to the oil industry, powerful voices in the American business community have been raised against any serious tax reforms. The American business press can always be counted on to issue the veiled threat that tax reform will lessen the industry's ardour in overcoming energy shortages.

The *Wall Street Journal* issued such a warning in January 1974: "The danger is that Congress, in swinging blindly, is apt to damage the nation's energy industry to an extent that will prolong the energy crisis indefinitely."

The *Journal* editorial then explained that oil company profits are the essential mechanism for creating capital pools for future energy development. It continued: "In announcing its $2.44 billion in profits yesterday, for example, Exxon also projected capital expenditures of $3.7 billion for 1974. The mechanism is working to get the United States out of the energy hole."[26]

The oil companies' acceptance of the new American strategy is no simple patriotic gesture. The oil companies have become too dependent on a single source of oil—the Middle East. Their capacity to play producing countries off against each other is potentially threatened by this. As noted earlier, the relationship between the oil companies and the OPEC countries must be understood as one both of struggle and of mutual cooperation. The new American energy strategy allows the oil companies to engage in a massive programme of capital investment during the seventies. The capital investment programme to be undertaken in North America will be financed out of the world-wide profits of the oil industry. The oil companies have set out to double the price of oil in relation to other commodities so that they can finance this enormous capital investment, as much as possible, out of their own internal operations. This way, they do not have to share their gigantic power with other capitalists.

The new American energy strategy also benefits American capitalism as a whole in its competition with its major rivals—Japan and western Europe. The American project of seeking self-sufficiency in energy is a viable one over the long run. But, for at least the remainder of this decade, large-scale imports of oil and natural gas will be essential for the United States. And there can be no doubt that the preferred source will be Canada. From now until at least 1985, it is reasonable to assume that the United States will want every barrel of oil and every cubic foot of natural gas that it can import from Canada. Or, as the *Wall Street Journal* put it:

> Energy czar William E. Simon and his aides talk of becoming "reasonably self-sufficient" by ending reliance on any "insecure" foreign sources (read: Arab) but they don't envision stopping imports from such "friendly" suppliers as Canada and Venezuela.[27]

Perhaps it is fitting that Exxon was most farsighted in understanding the change in strategy that was necessary. Between 1964 and 1967, while the other major companies were sitting on their existing reserves, Exxon spent $700 million exploring frantically for new sources of petroleum *outside the OPEC countries*. One of the key areas under exploration was the Mackenzie Delta in the Canadian Arctic, an area that Exxon had tied up by the end of the sixties.[28] Exxon's investment gamble into higher cost areas of the world is now beginning to pay off.

For Canada, America's dependent northern resource base, America's new energy strategy will have fateful implications. The response of Canada to it will determine Canada's industrial strategy and will have much to do with whether the Canadian nation can itself remain viable.

Notes

[1]*Congressional Quarterly,* September 7, 1973.

[2]*Congressional Quarterly,* November 10, 1973.

[3]*Congressional Quarterly,* April 28, 1973.

[4]*Congressional Quarterly,* April 21, 1973.

[5]*Ibid.*

[6]*Congressional Quarterly,* July 7, 1973.

[7]*Ibid.*

[8]*Congressional Quarterly,* November 24, 1973.

[9]*Ibid.*

[10]*Congressional Quarterly,* July 15, 1973.

[11]*Congressional Quarterly,* November 24, 1973.

[12]*Congressional Quarterly,* February 3, 1973.

[13]*Ibid.*

[14]*Ibid.*

[15]*Ibid.*

[16]Canada, Department of Energy, Mines and Resources report, *An Energy Policy for Canada—Phase I* (Ottawa, Department of Energy, Mines and Resources, 1973), v. 1, p. 133.

[17]James Laxer, "Canadian Manufacturing and U.S. Trade Policy", in Robert Laxer, ed., *(Canada) Ltd.,* (Toronto, McClelland and Stewart, 1973) p. 141.

[18]Peter R. Odell, *Oil and World Power* (London, Penguin, 1970) p. 44.

[19]Report of the OECD Oil Committee, *Oil: The Present Situation and Future Prospects* (Paris, Organization for Economic Cooperation and Development, 1973) p. 64.

[20]*New York Times,* February 14, 1974.

[21]*Ibid.*

[22]*Wall Street Journal,* November 16, 1973.

[23]OECD Oil Committee Report, *op. cit.,* pp. 153, 156.

[24]*Wall Street Journal,* January 15, 1974.

[25]*Wall Street Journal*, January 25, 1974.
[26]*Wall Street Journal*, January 26, 1974.
[27]*Wall Street Journal*, March 6, 1974.
[28]*Forbes*, February 15, 1973.

6 Canada's Energy Resources and Needs

Canada is not at present an oil-producing nation of world importance. Canadian oil production amounts to only about three per cent of total world production. What is significant about Canadian oil production is its record of rapid growth since 1960 and its potential for still more significant growth in the future.

Primary consumption of energy trebled in Canada between 1945 and the early 1970s. And, not surprisingly, the past quarter-century has seen a complete reordering of the proportions of fuels used. In 1945, coal was the source of 51.5 per cent of the nation's energy; by 1972, coal accounted for only 10 per cent of Canadian energy production. The same period saw a decrease from 10.5 to 1 per cent for wood as a source of the country's energy. Oil, natural gas and hydro all grew significantly in importance. Oil moved from supplying 18.5 to 44 per cent of the Canadian total; natural gas from 2.3 to 19.9 per cent; and hydro from 17.2 to 24.1 per cent. Nuclear energy appeared only in the 1970s, providing a mere 1 per cent of the nation's energy in 1972.[1]

The importance of energy production in the economy can be seen from the fact that in 1970 capital investment in power facilities and fuels amounted to $3.2 billion out of a total national capital investment for all industries of $17.8 billion. About half of this capital investment went into the electric power production industry, 47 per cent into the petroleum and natural gas industries and 3 per cent into the coal and uranium industries.[2]

Since 1960 Canada has switched from being a net importer to a net exporter of energy. In 1960 Canada's deficit in energy trade amounted to $300 million; by 1972 this had changed to a $634 million surplus.[3] The turnaround in Canada's energy trade is largely accounted for through the huge growth in Canada's oil and natural gas exports. Canada's oil exports quadrupled from 252 thousand barrels of crude oil and oil products a day in 1962 to 1144 thousand barrels a day in 1972. During this same ten year period, imports of crude oil and oil products only doubled from 452 thousand barrels a day to 909 thousand barrels.[4] During these years natural gas exports trebled from 343 billion cubic feet in 1962 to 1,012 billion cubic feet in 1972 (natural gas imports are inconsequential). Canadian exports of oil and natural gas have gone entirely to the United States, while oil imports have mainly come from Venezuela and the Middle East.

In 1972 Canada imported 389 thousand barrels of crude oil daily from Venezuela; 98 thousand barrels from Iran; 73 thousand barrels from Saudi Arabia and 58 thousand barrels from Nigeria. Other sources included the Trucial States, Iraq, Libya, Colombia, Trinidad and Kuwait.[5]

In addition to mushrooming exports of oil and natural gas, Canada had a small surplus in its trade in electrical power with the United States. In 1972 Canada's net exports of electric power to the U.S. amounted to 3.3 per cent of total Canadian electric power generated.[6]

While Canada has become a large net exporter of energy to the United States, it continues to import significant amounts of coal from that country. In 1972, even though Canada produced 20.6 million tons of coal (mostly in Alberta and British Columbia), and exported 9.4 million tons (mostly to Japan), this country imported 19.3 million tons of coal from the United States, mainly for use in generating electric power in Ontario and the Maritimes and for the steel industry in Ontario.[7]

In terms of oil, the Canadian market has been divided into two regions since the establishment of the national oil policy in 1961. The 1961 decision guaranteed that the Canadian market west of the Ottawa Valley would purchase only domestic oil production, over three-quarters of which comes from Alberta. East of the Ottawa Valley the market was to be supplied from overseas sources, mainly Venezuela and the Middle East. In terms of pricing, this meant higher cost oil for Ontario and the West than for eastern Canada until the current round of price increases in the OPEC countries. The sixties was the period of mandatory oil import quotas in the United States and the Canadian crude oil price was set in relation to crude oil prices in the markets of the American Northwest.

Almost without warning Canada's national oil policy has been reduced to ruins as a result of the world oil crisis. Canadians are now being told that the days of cheap and plentiful energy are over. The future, we are told, lies in expensive non-conventional fuel sources that must soon replace our fast-depleting conventional petroleum supplies.

Just how large are Canada's petroleum resources in terms of Canadian and foreign demand?

Information on reserves is drawn from two major sources: the estimates of the petroleum companies themselves and the estimates of government agencies. In its June 1973 energy report, the Department of Energy, Mines and Resources relied on estimates made by the oil industry and provincial and federal government agencies.

A cautionary word is in order on the predictive value of previous government studies of expected energy resource developments. The 1973 report is to be congratulated on its frank modesty concerning the likely accuracy of forecasts. The report quotes from the predictions of Canada's 1946 Royal Commission on Coal, the chairman of which wrote that "despite the importance of alternative sources of energy, coal is and will probably continue to be, the most important source of energy for railway locomotives and industrial and domestic heating." Considering that coal supplied over half of the nation's energy at the time the report was written and that this has now fallen to 10 per cent, it is obvious that the predictive value of the Royal Commission was nil.[8]

It is also important to note that many Canadian geologists are highly critical of the way reserves are now estimated. Armed with this perspective it is possible to look at estimates of the nation's reserves without regarding them as the final truth on the subject.

In December 1972, the Canadian Petroleum Association estimated that Canada's conventional oil reserves stood at 9.7 billion barrels of remaining crude oil and gas liquids, with all but .2 billion barrels of this reserve existing in western Canada and over 75 per cent of this reserve located in Alberta. Natural gas reserves amounted to 52.9 trillion cubic feet, all but 1.6 trillion of this from western Canada, again mainly in Alberta. In terms of the annual production rate for 1972, Canada had 15 years of proven reserves of oil, down from 24.5 years of proven reserves of oil in 1966, prior to the recent enormous increase in output. Natural gas reserves stood at about 25 years' supply in terms of 1972 output.[9]

These figures detail Canada's *proven* reserves as estimated by the oil industry (the Canadian Petroleum Association is an industry spokesman); what then are the *potential* reserves of these fuels?

In 1972 the Geological Survey of Canada (a federal government agency), began to make annual estimates of Canada's probable petroleum reserves. Its first two projections, for 1972 (Estimate I) and for 1973 (Estimate II), are the basis of discussion of the nation's long-term petroleum resources in the government's energy report.

The GSC's Estimate I is considerably more optimistic than its Estimate II. The two estimates differ significantly respecting conventional oil. Estimate I predicts that Canada's conventional oil reserves (recoverable without economic or technological restraints), less today's proven reserves, stands at 118 billion barrels. Estimate II drops this figure to 83 billion barrels.

The key difference in the two estimates concerns conventional oil reserves in the Canadian Arctic, with Estimate II predicting a northern reserve of 28 billion barrels, less than half of Estimate I, which predicted 70 billion barrels. This drop is somewhat offset by the upward revision of the east coast potential from 42 to 50 billion barrels.

Of key importance is the fact that both Estimate I and Estimate II see only small remaining unproven conventional reserves in Canada's traditional petroleum production centre, the Prairies. Thus, both estimates point to exploration for conventional reserves shifting away from Alberta to the Canadian Arctic and the east coast.[10]

According to Estimate I, Canada has a potential reserve of 180 years' supply of conventional crude in terms of the 1972 level of production. Estimate II drops this potential to 120 years' supply. (Naturally, if annual production doubles or trebles, the life-expectancy of the reserve declines accordingly).

The GSC's second estimate is also more pessimistic than its first regarding Canada's natural gas potential. In the case of natural gas though, the downward revision is not as significant as for oil. Recoverable potential reserves of natural gas, less proven reserves, are placed at 712 trillion cubic feet in Estimate II, down from the 835 trillion cubic feet predicted in Estimate I. Here the sharpest reduction comes in the estimate for western Canada, which in Estimate II is 44 trillion cubic feet, down from 101 trillion cubic feet in Estimate I.[11]

If the more optimistic estimate is correct, Canada's potential natural gas reserves would be good for 400 years at the 1972 level of output, 350 years if the more pessimistic estimate is correct.

In addition to conventional petroleum reserves, Canada has large non-conventional reserves in the form of oil sands and heavy oils. Oil sands consist of a highly viscous, bitumen-like crude oil mixed with sand. Deposits of oil sands exist in surface outcrops and down to depths of 2,000 feet. Tar-like in consistency, the oil does not flow, and for recovery must either be mined or be induced to flow by the injection of heat or solvents.[12]

Heavy oils are a transitional form between oil sands and conventional oil. They are highly viscous and require the injection of heat or solvents to bring about normal flow.[13]

The Alberta oil sands (or Athabasca tar sands as they are alternatively called), are estimated by the Oil and Gas Conservation Board of

Alberta to contain 301 billion barrels of recoverable oil. According to this estimate, sixty-five billion barrels of this reserve are recoverable through open-pit mining techniques now in existence, while the remaining 236 billion barrels must be extracted through "In-situ" recovery techniques.[14] "In-situ" recovery means literally "in place" recovery—the separation of the oil from the sand in place, resulting in the recovery of the oil at the surface with the sand remaining in the reservoir.[15] "In-situ" recovery of oil depends on the development of technology not now available.

The importance of the oil sands can be seen from the fact that the recoverable reserve there represents 450 years' supply of oil at the 1972 level of Canadian output. The recoverable portion of the oil sands alone is half the size of the world's present proven reserves of conventional oil.

In addition to the problem of estimating reserves, it is also necessary to estimate the cost at which these reserves would become available. The same problem exists for estimates of cost as for amount: the oil industry is the main source of information, and its estimates are highly suspect, because of its vested interest in those estimates. Not everyone is as forthright as the Shah of Iran, who recently declared that the cost of producing a barrel of oil in Iran is eleven cents. He went on to say that his return on a barrel now stands at $7.00; therefore, he concluded, anyone charging you more than $7.11 a barrel for Iranian crude oil is taking his own profit from it.

Reserve estimates, to be meaningful, are always presented in terms of the cost per barrel involved in their extraction. It makes little sense to place oil that is twice as costly to produce in the same category as oil that is available at half the cost. The federal government's energy report presents estimates of the costs at which the nation's reserves would become available. The problem with its estimated "costs" is that they are actually "prices" with profits for the oil companies built into them.

The cost estimates in the report are not actually itemized estimates of the costs of exploring, developing and producing petroleum—they are estimates of the price the oil industry will charge to produce petroleum. All of the prices include what the report calls "a reasonable rate of return" on the investment of the companies.

The report's estimate of what a reasonable rate of return ought to be is obscured by its division of returns into two categories, "profits" and "rents". The report states that a 20 per cent rate of *profit* on capital invested should be regarded as reasonable.[16] But, the report explains, over and above the costs of exploration, production and transportation, and a "reasonable rate of return", there may be a considerable "rent" that can be collected to bring the price up to prevailing international levels. The term "rent" is a euphemism here for "windfall profit". Significantly, the report concludes that the federal and provincial governments at present collect only a small proportion of this "rent" in comparison with the amount collected by governments in other countries.

Using the larger GSC estimate on Canadian reserves, the report concludes that over the next half-century the value of this economic "rent" on Canada's oil and natural gas will be between twenty and thirty billion dollars.[17] (Again, this is in addition to the reasonable profit rate of 20 per cent.) A great issue to be settled, in the view of this report, is how much of this rent should go to the oil companies, how much to the government, and how much to the consumer in the form of lower prices. Under present conditions, most of it will go to the oil industry.

The oil industry does not like to talk about its actual rate of return on the sale of a barrel of crude oil, and government reports also regard this as an impolite subject. However, it is possible to break down the cost of producing a barrel of crude oil and estimate the rate of return to the industry. This calculation will help us to estimate what the actual costs of producing oil will be in the future.

According to *Oilweek* magazine, the average cost of producing a barrel of Canadian crude oil between 1966 and 1970 was as follows: exploration, $.20; development drilling, $.08; land, $.16; producing facilities. $.09; lifting, $.27; royalties, $.30; taxes $.14. Total, $1.24. In 1966, the average wellhead price of western Canadian crude oil was $2.39; in 1970, $2.77.[18] Therefore, the industry profit on a barrel of oil was $1.15 in 1966; $1.53 in 1970. During these years the industry's wellhead price was double its costs.

If the federal government's energy report is based on the same assumed rate of return (there is no reason to believe that it is not), then the price estimates in it actually break down as follows: 50 per cent of the estimate represents costs; 50 per cent goes to the industry. This ratio should be remembered when oil development costs are considered.

Keeping in mind that the following figures should be divided in half to calculate the actual costs, let us examine the energy report's estimates about the prices at which reserves would become available. (All of the following prices are expressed in constant 1972 dollars.) The nation's conventional oil reserves were assumed to be recoverable at present market prices (present meaning June 1973, when Canadian crude prices were about $3.50 a barrel). The report concludes that at June 1973 prices, not enough oil would become available in the Canadian Arctic to justify the construction of a pipeline southward. But at $5.00 a barrel, approximately 50 billion barrels would become available in the frontier areas, according to GSC Estimate I, and 25 billion barrels, according to Estimate II. At $8.00 a barrel the potential for these new sources of conventional crude could reach almost 70 billion barrels (Estimate I) or almost 40 billion barrels (Estimate II).[19]

The report estimates that of the 65 billion barrels in the Alberta oil sands that can be extracted through open-pit mining methods, 15 billion barrels would be available for $5.00 a barrel and 35 billion barrels at $6.00 a barrel. Heavy oil costs were estimated at between $5.00 and $8.00 a barrel.[20]

As for natural gas, the report estimates that 250 trillion cubic feet would become available at $1.25 per thousand cubic feet and that at $1.60 per thousand cubic feet a total of 450 trillion cubic feet would become available. The current price at the time of the report was 40 to 45 cents per thousand cubic feet in the Great Lakes area of Canada.[21]

Having reviewed the available information about the supply of oil and natural gas, what can we say about the projected demand for Canadian energy resources?

This question is, if anything, even more loaded politically than the question of petroleum reserves. The answer varies enormously depending on the type of society one aspires to, or expects to see, in Canada. Predictably, the federal government's June 1973 energy report bases its projection for Canadian demand on the assumption that Canadian society will not alter qualitatively between now and the year 2000. The report sets out this projection for energy demand and energy supply for the year 2000 in Canada:

> Assuming no major changes in government policies or Canadian attitudes towards energy use or conservation, Canada's primary energy requirement by the year 2000 is likely to be more than four times that of today. Based on a population estimate of 35 million in the year 2000 our per capita energy consumption would be 2.7 times that of 1970. Only minor increases in the efficiency of energy use are assumed in this forecast. Increasing prices for energy commodities will tend to moderate demand growth rates in the long run.
>
> The forms of energy used directly by the consumer (secondary energy) in the year 2000 will not differ markedly from today; petroleum and natural gas will probably still account for almost 80 per cent, coal will drop from 6 per cent to 2 per cent and electricity will meet the remaining 18 to 20 per cent. The sources of power for electricity generation, however, will change significantly. Hydroelectric power is expected to decline to 30 per cent in 2000 while nuclear power will increase to some 44 per cent from 0.5 per cent in

1970. Thus, by the end of the century, nuclear power will provide more than 8 per cent of our total secondary energy consumption compared to much less than 1 per cent today.

There is considerable uncertainty about future energy consumption patterns. Changes in life styles of Canadians, changes in the economic structure of the nation, and government policies relating to the environment or conservation can have an important impact on energy demand. The consumption forecast could be 15 per cent higher or 25 per cent lower than the standard forecast for the year 2000 depending on these factors. The range could be even wider if economic growth or population levels are far different from standard projections. [22]

The report goes on to make a longer term prediction of energy demand and supply for Canada to the year 2050. In that year Canada will have an "electrical society" with 90 per cent of energy coming in the form of electricity.

As for fossil fuels the report sees them beginning to decline in Canadian use in the period 2020 to 2030. [23]

Having estimated Canadian petroleum supply and domestic demand, the report draws the following conclusions about the availability of Canadian oil for domestic use: "It is evident . . . that Canada should not physically run out of oil. The volumes of oil that can be made available from synthetic sources are so large that there is little question that Canada can satisfy her own needs easily until the year 2050 at oil prices reaching $7 or $8." [24]

The report also predicts Canada's possible surplus of oil and gas, which could be exported. It states: "Oil and gas resource Estimate I suggests that Canada may have an enormous potential surplus above its own requirements. In the case of Estimate II this estimated surplus has diminished considerably, from about 5 million barrels a day surplus capacity in the year 2000 to about 1½ million barrels a day." [25]

Based on these assessments of demand and supply of Canadian oil and gas, the report concludes that between now and the year 2000 Canadian exports of oil and natural gas could range between providing from zero to 12 per cent of U.S. demand. [26] At present, Canada supplies about 6 per cent of U.S. oil needs and about 3 per cent of its natural gas needs.

The report's estimates of Canadian supply and demand make it clear that this country has an adequate supply of conventional oil and natural gas, available at low cost for domestic needs. With supplements from more costly oil sands production and offshore production of oil and gas in the Atlantic region, domestic supply should be assured. However, to go beyond supplying domestic use, that is, the production of Arctic oil and gas and extensive oil sands development for export markets, would mean drawing on reserves that would be much more costly to produce.

Notes

[1]Canada, Department of Energy, Mines and Resources report, *An Energy Policy for Canada—Phase I* (Ottawa, Department of Energy, Mines and Resources, 1973), v. 1, p. 32.

[2]*Ibid.*, p. 36.

[3]*Ibid.*, p. 35.

[4]*Ibid.*, p. 38.

[5]Canadian Petroleum Association, *1972 Statistical Year Book* (Calgary, Canadian Petroleum Association, 1973) p. 93.

[6]Canada, Department of Energy Report, *op. cit.*, v. 1, p. 8.

[7]*Ibid.*

[8]*Ibid.*, v. 1, p. 62.

[9]*Ibid.*, v. 1, p. 8.

[10]*Ibid.*, v. 1, p. 87.

[11]*Ibid.*, v. 1, p. 89.

[12]*Ibid.*, v. 1, p. 8.

[13]*Ibid.*, v. 1, p. 7.

[14]*Ibid.*, v. 1, p. 87.

[15]*Ibid.*, v. 1, p. 8.

[16]*Ibid.*, v. 1, p. 82.

[17]*Ibid.*, v. 1, p. 152.

[18]Statistics from *Oilweek,* February 21, 1972 and Canadian Petroleum Association, *op. cit.*, p. 61.

[19]Canada, Department of Energy Report, v. 1, p. 90.

[20]*Ibid.*

[21]*Ibid.*, v. 1, p. 94.

[22]*Ibid.*, v. 1, p. 11.

[23]*Ibid.*, v. 1, p. 99.

[24]*Ibid.*, v. 1, p. 104.

[25]*Ibid.*, v. 1, p. 101.
[26]*Ibid.*, v. 1, p. 127.

7 Canada's Branch-plant Oil Industry

The Canadian oil industry is a miniature replica of the world oil industry. Its ownership, its technology, its policies, and its crises have all spilled over into Canada from abroad.

Almost 30 per cent of all foreign investment is centered in the country's petroleum industry,[1] in 1970 this amounted to $9.8 billion. Over 91 per cent of the assets and over 95 per cent of the industry's sales are accounted for by foreign-owned firms. Foreign control of the vertically integrated firms, which carry on activities in all aspects of the industry, is one hundred per cent. And these vertically integrated firms account for $5.5 billion or 51 per cent of the petroleum industry's assets.[2]

As in the United States, the petroleum industry in Canada has been moving to broaden its holdings in energy resources other than oil and gas. For example, during the past decade, foreign control of Canada's coal industry has grown rapidly and has reached the 73 per cent mark.[3]

Eighty per cent of the foreign ownership in Canada's petroleum industry is American.[4]

The firms which dominate the world oil business are also the firms which run the Canadian petroleum industry. Perhaps it is then appropriate that pre-eminence in Canada's oil industry should be vested in Imperial Oil Limited, the subsidiary of that majestic giant of world oil, the Exxon Corporation. Exxon owns 69.7 per cent of the capital stock in Imperial Oil, one of Exxon's several hundred subsidiaries around the world. In turn, Imperial is a holding company which controls 49 companies in Canada, according to Statistics Canada data.[5]

As the *Financial Post* describes Imperial's operations:

[This] Company, together with its subsidiaries, comprises a fully integrated oil enterprise and is the largest such unit in Canada. Engages either directly or through subsidiaries in exploration for and production of crude oil, natural gas and gas by-products, transports crude by ocean-going and lake tankers, pipeline and tank cars, operates nine refineries and distributes and markets petroleum products in every province in Canada as well as the Northwest Territories. Chemicals, fertilizers and a wide range of building products are also manufactured and marketed.

Imperial Oil Limited has been engaged in the manufacture and sale of chemicals since 1957 and is, at present, the largest supplier of basic and intermediate organic chemicals in Canada.[6]

In addition to these traditional activities, Imperial is moving into other fields designed to enhance its "total" impact on the economy. One such venture, being undertaken in conjunction with S.B. McLaughlin Associates Limited, involves Imperial in the development of Mississauga Valleys, an urban project west of Metropolitan Toronto. This new concept in city development stars the oil company in the roles of financier, builder and provider of fuel.

In return for providing a five million dollar loan and further funding of up to ten million dollars, Imperial gets to fuel the homes with Esso oil, install its hot water heaters in the homes, and provide ten million dollars' worth of building materials such as vinyl siding, roofing paper and floor tiles through its wholly owned subsidiary, Building Products of Canada Ltd. In addition, the lucky people of Mississauga Valleys will be able to fill their gas tanks at handy Esso service stations, drawn right into the community development plan.[7]

Income from Imperial's operations totalled a staggering $2,045 million in 1972. This means that roughly 2 per cent of all expenditures made in Canada in 1972 were made to this one firm. Its operating income was greater than the general revenues of eight of Canada's ten provincial governments. Imperial's profits in 1972 were $151 million. And in the first nine months of 1973 Imperial had improved on this with profits already running at $155 million—up 46 per cent over the first three-quarters of 1972. But, for a real appreciation of the company's good fortune, it should be noted that the third quarter alone saw a profit of $60 million, up 100 per cent over the $30 million profit made in the third quarter of 1972.[8]

Imperial produced an average of 224,000 barrels of crude oil and gas liquids daily in 1972, over one-eighth of the national total. Its refineries processed 399,000 barrels of crude a day, and its sales of petroleum products amounted to 417,000 barrels daily, each of these figures representing about 25 per cent of the national total.[9]

For some years, Imperial has been heavily involved in Arctic oil and gas exploration, particularly in the Mackenzie Delta.[10] The oil company also has a 30 per cent interest in Syncrude Canada Ltd., which was formed in 1965 to come up with a plan for extracting oil from the Alberta oil sands. Syncrude has now embarked on a billion-dollar venture to establish a plant that would begin production in 1978.[11]

Imperial's domination of the Canadian oil industry can be appreciated from the fact that its operations outdistance the combined activities of its next two competitors, Shell and Gulf. Canada's second and third largest oil companies are almost identical in their sales levels: $867 million for Shell and $851 million for Gulf in 1972.[12]

Shell's production of crude oil and natural gas liquids averaged 92,000 barrels a day in the first nine months of 1973. The company refined 270,000 barrels of oil per day during the same period. In 1972 Shell's profits were $78 million in Canada, an increase of 28 per cent over 1971.[13]

Gulf produced 151,000 barrels of oil and gas liquids on a daily average in the first six months of 1973, while refining 282,000 barrels daily. Gulf's 1972 profit of $64 million was an increase of 21 per cent over the 1971 total.[14]

Both Shell and Gulf, like Imperial, are fully integrated petroleum companies with activities in the Arctic, the oil sands and offshore exploration.

Texaco Canada Ltd. is next in size with annual sales of $455 million in 1972. The company's crude oil and liquid gas production averaged 32,000 barrels a day in 1972, with refinery runs of 146,000 barrels a day. Profits in 1972 totalled $42 million, up 35 per cent from 1971.[15]

Many Canadians accept the control of the Canadian oil industry by these foreign firms in the belief that foreign ownership is a necessary evil in industries like oil, which require huge amounts of capital investment.

The assumption is that a large inflow of foreign risk capital makes possible the development of Canada's energy resources. In fact, little risk is involved—the nation's foreign-owned petroleum companies have been generating an increasing percentage of their investment funds from their Canadian operations. In the period 1961-65, foreign-owned petroleum firms in Canada generated 57.6 per cent of their capital from their own internal operations; in the years 1966-70 this rose to 73.8 per cent. In the early sixties direct foreign contributions to the capital funds of foreign-owned oil companies amounted to 26 per cent of the total; in the late sixties foreign sources supplied only 17.6 per cent of the capital.[16]

In the early sixties, the outflow of dividends to the foreign owners of the oil companies had amounted to only 11.2 per cent of profits, less than half of the inflow of new foreign capital during these years.

But by the late sixties the outflow of dividends to foreign owners reached 18.1 per cent of surplus funds spent, surpassing the inflow of new foreign capital.[17]

Therefore, by the end of the sixties, Canadians were financing their own oil industry, although its growth meant higher and higher profits for foreigners rather than for Canadians. Furthermore, by the end of the sixties, government tax write-offs in the form of depletion allowances, depreciation, deferred taxes (and others) supplied the foreign-owned companies with more of their capital than any other source—a staggering 38.4 per cent.[18]

This meant that the Canadian people were already contributing more to the capital pools of the oil companies, in the form of taxes forgone, than were the companies' book profits. Without gaining a nickel's worth of equity value for this investment, the Canadian people were putting up twice as much investment capital as were the foreign owners of the oil companies.

Notes

[1]Canada, Department of Energy, Mines and Resources report, *An Energy Policy for Canada—Phase I* (Ottawa, Department of Energy, Mines and Resources, 1973), v. 1, p. 22.

[2]*Ibid.*, v. 1, p. 240.

[3]*Ibid.*, v. 1, p. 20.

[4]*Ibid.*

[5]Statistics Canada, *Inter-Corporate Ownership 1969* (Ottawa, Information Canada, 1971) pp. 504-505.

[6]Data card for Imperial Oil Ltd., August 10, 1973, compiled by the Financial Post Corporation Service, Toronto.

[7]*Ibid.*

[8]Imperial Oil Ltd. data card, December 5, 1973, *op. cit.*

[9]Imperial Oil Ltd. data card, August 10, 1973, *op. cit.*

[10]*Ibid.*

[11]*Ibid.*

[12]Statistics from data card for Shell Canada Ltd., December 3, 1973, and data card for Gulf Oil Canada Ltd., October 29, 1973, compiled by the Financial Post Corporation Service, Toronto.

[13]Statistics from Shell Canada Ltd. data card for July 10, 1972 and Gulf Oil Canada Ltd. data card for July 19, 1972, *op. cit.*

[14]*Ibid.*

[15]Data card for Texaco Canada Ltd., October 19, 1973, compiled by the Financial Post Corporation Service, Toronto.

[16]Canada, Department of Energy Report, *op. cit.*, v.1, pp. 242-243.

[17]*Ibid.*

[18]*Ibid.*

8

Canadian Energy Policy: The Emergence of a Continental Energy Strategy

The development of a significant petroleum industry in Canada has occurred under the control of the foreign-owned oil companies. The evolution of Canada's national oil policy and the growth of its oil and natural gas exports have taken place in response to the needs of these foreign corporations.

Over the past decade, Canada has been evolving an energy policy that assumes that the export of energy resources to the U.S. is essential to the health of the Canadian economy. For Canadian governments, Liberal or Conservative, presiding over a branch-plant economy, resource exports continue to be seen as the key mechanism for generating economic growth and for paying for imports of American manufactured products.

American branch plant corporations run both Canada's resource and manufacturing industries. Since World War II, American control of commodity production has meant that the economic strategy of Canadian governments has reflected the needs of these dominant foreign-owned corporations.

As noted in a previous chapter, when the U.S. adopted voluntary import controls in the early 1950s, the federal government treated some foreign sources of oil for the United States as more reliable than others. The only country to be exempted from the Eisenhower mandatory import controls of 1959 was Canada.

During the sixties Canadian energy policy and this country's petroleum industry were developed as extensions of the American mandatory import quota system. The American system, which evolved to protect American domestic production from cheap overseas crude oil imports, had the effect of dividing the capitalist world into two great zones with respect to price: the United States and the rest of the capitalist world. Since Canadian petroleum production was exempt from the U.S. import quotas, its reference price had to be the American price of crude oil—otherwise its unlimited admission to the American market would have undercut the price of American crude. If the reference price of Canadian crude was to be the American and not the world price, then the Canadian market also had to be protected from cheaper overseas imports. Thus, the necessity of extending the American quota system northward under its Canadian brand name —the national oil policy.

Proclaimed in 1961 by the Diefenbaker government, the national oil policy did not set up a complex import quota system as had the United States. Instead, Canada was divided into two regions; western Canada and Ontario were to be on the American side of the price wall, while the country east of the Ottawa Valley was to be subject to the international price of oil. Both regions were a part of the American oil empire, but one was treated as a part of United States domestic operations, while the other was accorded foreign market status. A graphic illustration of the inclusion of western Canada and Ontario in United States domestic operations is the fact that the Interprovincial Pipeline, which supplies Ontario with western Canadian oil, ignores international boundaries and runs south of the Great Lakes, delivering oil to the American North- and Mid-west as it goes.

What was effectively a continental energy policy quickly branched out into energy fields other than petroleum and soon gained a bi-partisan character under the subsequent Liberal governments of Pearson and Trudeau. At the same time as the northward extension of the American import system was being Canadianized as the "national" oil policy, the Diefenbaker government, and later the Pearson government, was selling the Columbia River to the United States as a source of cheap hydro power for the state of Washington.

The Columbia River Treaty, which meant the abandonment of the principle of separate national development of the boundary waters on either side of the Canada-U.S. frontier, embodied instead the concept of north-south regional resource development without respect to the border, the same approach that was being taken to oil.[1]

The Columbia River case served as the model for the evolution of official thinking on the subject of continental energy resource development. This approach was elaborated in the Merchant-Heeney report of 1965. The Merchant-Heeney report was produced by the former U.S. ambassador to Canada and the former Canadian ambassador to Washington, following discussions between Prime Minister Lester Pearson and U.S. President Lyndon Johnson in the U.S. capital in January 1964. The Prime Minister and the President charged Merchant and Heeney "with the task of examining the desirability and practicability of developing acceptable principles which would make it easier to avoid divergencies in economic and other policies of interest to each other.''[2]

At the time of its publication, the feature of the Merchant-Heeney report that received the most public attention was the recommendation that Canada restrict itself to quiet diplomacy in its relations with the United States, avoiding public disagreement as much as possible. The report stated:

> It is important and reasonable that Canadian authorities should have careful regard for the United States Government's position in . . . [the] world context, and, in the absence of special Canadian interests and obligations, avoid so far as possible, public disagreement especially upon critical issues.[3]

Behind this conclusion in the report was a whole rationale for the way in which the Canadian and American governments should deal with each other. In general, Merchant and Heeney called for an approach to Canadian-American relations that would treat important questions more as technical matters than as political questions. The report called for the following general method of procedure:

> In certain fields where combined efforts are called for, such as continental air defence arrangements and joint development of resources, there is obvious advantage in having the consultative process begin at the planning stage so as to facilitate concurrent formulation of policy.[4]

The report was explicit about the need to move toward a continental approach to the development of energy resources, particularly in the case of electrical energy. It referred to ''the economic advantages to both countries of disregarding the boundary for energy purposes, that is, in the development and distribution of energy on a regional north-south basis where this is to the mutual advantage.'' The report did not limit itself to a discussion of electrical energy alone, but concluded that ''we believe there would be virtue in having a joint look at the energy picture as a whole.''[5]

One enthusiastic advocate of resource development on a north-south basis has been Jack Austin, the present deputy minister of Canada's Department of Energy, Mines and Resources. For him the model to emulate was the Columbia River Treaty, whose example had inspired Merchant and Heeney in their report.

In a speech in 1969, Austin said, ''While no general principles may have been established in law as a result of its language, certainly we hope that the practice of resource sharing as explained in the Columbia River Treaty, is an indication of the tendency of the same parties to deal with other resource problems in the same way."[6]

The man who drew most public attention with his advocacy of a continental energy deal, and later with his attempts to disown the concept, was former Energy Minister J.J. Greene. In December 1969, at a press conference in Washington, Greene declared himself in favour of a continental energy resources deal so that "people will benefit, and both countries will benefit, irrespective of where the imaginary border goes."[7]

Greene's Washington remarks came just at the time Americans began to be concerned about the domestic supply of natural gas. In February 1970, the U.S. government's Shultz report called for a "harmonized energy policy" with Canada. The justification for this was the security value of Canadian supplies.

The report stated: "The risk of political instability or animosity is generally conceded to be very low in Canada. The risk of physical interruption or diversion of Canadian oil to other export markets in an emergency is also minimal for those deliveries made by inland transport."[8]

But the Shultz report was not completely satisfied with Canada as a source of petroleum imports. Since the Arab-Israeli War of 1967, American oil planners had been increasingly concerned about the possibility of oil boycotts. Canada was seen by the authors of the Shultz report as a source of secure petroleum, which could be counted on to assist in undercutting any Arab oil boycott. But this meant that the Canadian national oil policy, so faithfully tailored to the American context in the sixties, would have to be altered. The problem was that Canada's dependency on imports of crude oil to supply its domestic market east of the Ottawa Valley undercut the security value of American imports of western Canadian crude. The report warned:

A large U.S. tariff preference for Canadian oil is difficult to justify while Eastern Canada continues to import all of its requirements from potentially insecure sources. In case of a supply interruption, Canada could be expected to turn to the United States to furnish those imports, or to compete for whatever supply is available, and thereby to subtract from the security value of U.S. imports from Western Canada. Some provision for limiting or offsetting Canadian vulnerability to an interruption of its own oil imports should therefore be made a precondition to unrestricted entry of Canadian oil into our market. Full realization of the security benefits implicit in such a preferential arrangement is also dependent on the development of common or harmonized United States-Canadian policies with respect to pipeline and other modes of transportation, access to natural gas, and other related energy matters. Pending the outcome of discussions on these subjects, the United States must decide what arrangements it is prepared to make unilaterally.[9]

In effect, the Shultz report was calling on Canada to extend the Interprovincial Oil Pipeline east from Ontario to Montreal to supply the eastern Canadian market with western Canadian crude. Only then could the U.S. allow full-scale entry of Canadian crude into the American market.

The American government moved quickly and clumsily a month later to attempt to muscle Canada into a formal energy pact. The chief U.S. desire at the time was for large-scale increases in imports of Canadian natural gas on a long-term basis. The Nixon administration, not yet faced with oil supply problems, decided to cut down the flow of Canadian crude to the U.S. market to bring the Canadian government speedily to terms. In March 1970, the U.S. imposed a quota on Canadian crude oil imports, cutting them back to 395,000 barrels a day. Two months later, the White House explained that the quota was aimed at pressuring Canada into a long-term energy arrangement.[10]

The cumulative effect of these events—Greene's call for a continental energy deal and Nixon's arm-twisting quota on Canadian oil imports—made a bad impression on the Canadian public. Already sensitized to the potentially explosive foreign ownership issue, the Liberal government was forced to do some fancy manoeuvring to avert a political disaster that would imperil the development of Canada's continental energy policy. The angry response from many quarters in Canada to Joe Greene's openly continentalist rhetoric revealed to Greene that he was in danger of ending up cast as villain in another 1956-style pipeline debate.

At his address to the Independent Petroleum Association of America in Denver, Colorado, Greene adjusted his rhetoric. He pointed out the maladroit character of the American effort to force Canada into an energy deal by clamping down on imports of Canadian oil. He complained about the political difficulty with the folks back home created by the U.S. quota:

> The unilateral action on quotas has created for us grave political problems which I am very sure were not considered by U.S. officials who recommended the arbitrary shut-off and restrictions. Canadian public opinion is interpreting this as a pressure play, to squeeze Canada into some form of energy deal which would not be to the Canadian advantage.[11]

In addition to warning the Americans to change the *style* of their diplomacy, Greene made two substantive points at Denver. Responding to the fact that the most pressing concern of the Americans was for additional natural gas imports, Greene said:

> ... Canadian gas will be available to supplement United States supplies only if our petroleum industry as a whole receives the incentives of progressive growth and assured stability of access to export markets for oil and natural gas liquids.[12]

In other words, Greene was using Canadian natural gas as a wedge for opening up the American market to Canadian oil, hardly a reversal of his continentalist approach!

His other substantive point came in the form of a reply to the Shultz report's suggestion that Canada do something about the security of supplies of oil in the eastern Canadian market. Greene reminded his audience:

> It must be left to *us*, to Canada, to evaluate the matter of oil supply security in eastern Canada and to take any appropriate action.
> This aspect of freedom of domestic policy-making is most important to us. We believe our national and international, political and economic circumstances are such that we must retain freedom to apply the Canadian solutions to Canadian problems.[13]

Greene was saying three things at Denver: first, that the U.S. must change the manner of its diplomatic approach to Canada if it wanted to get anywhere on energy matters; second, that additional natural gas exports depended on guaranteed access for Canadian oil to the American market; and finally, that the security of eastern Canadian oil imports was a Canadian, not an American problem. How has the government lived up to Joe Green's demands and pledges at Denver? One success, and two failures.

First, the success. The Canadian government has convinced Washington to change the *style* of its diplomatic relationship with Canada. Confirmation of this came from the highest level in the spring of 1972, when President Nixon visited Ottawa. In his address to the Canadian Parliament, Nixon declared that Canada is an independent country with its own distinctive national identity. This may seem a trivial matter. But for a government that has lost real control over its national economy to foreign corporations and a foreign state, issues of style become very important. That the Canadian government has been perfectly willing to proceed with the *substance* of a continental energy policy is evident from the fact that between 1961 and 1972 the proportion of Canadian oil being exported to the U.S. increased from 21 per cent to over 50 per cent.[14] However, it is essential that Ottawa retain the *appearance* of a sovereign government. Thus, the oddity of having the head of state of a foreign country declare us independent. Even Nixon must have found this one of his strangest tasks.

Now the failures. Greene pledged that Canada would not sell additional natural gas to the United States until the oil import quota was removed. But in September 1970, while the oil import quota was still in place, the Canadian government approved the largest natural gas deal in this country's history. Canada agreed to sell 6.3 trillion cubic feet of natural gas to the U.S. over the next fifteen to twenty years for a price of about two billion dollars.[15]

What about Greene's declaration that the security of eastern Canadian oil supplies was none of the business of the United States? Greene's successor as energy minister, Donald Macdonald, admitted in January 1973 that he had been engaging in secret negotiations with the U.S. on the security of eastern Canada's oil supply.[16]

Even without any formal agreement committing Canada to a continental energy policy, the pace of Canadian exports of oil continued to increase more rapidly than did domestic consumption of Canadian oil. In 1961, the year the national oil policy was initiated, exports to the U.S. of crude oil and natural gas liquids averaged 185,000 barrels a day, while Canadian consumption of Canadian crude and liquids averaged 409,900 barrels a day. In 1971, for the first time, more Canadian crude and liquids were exported to the U.S. than were consumed in Canada. And in 1973, the year of the "energy crisis", the pace of exports continued to climb, reaching 1,175,000 barrels a day compared with 805,000 barrels of Canadian crude and liquids consumed by Canadians.[17]

As the pace of Canadian exports increased, debate about Canada's continental energy policy mounted. The government was the object of criticism for its failure to define a clear and coherent energy strategy.

In June 1973, in a political atmosphere of growing concern about the future direction of Canadian energy policy, the Department of Energy, Mines and Resources published its long-awaited two volume report, entitled *An Energy Policy for Canada*. While the report mainly analyses the nature of Canada's energy industries, and projects future conditions respecting price, supply and demand (as discussed in Chapter 6), it does indicate the general direction of federal government policy preferences.

The energy report outlines five models upon which Canadian energy development could be based for the remainder of this decade.

Case A, Self-sufficient Development, assumes that there will be no further extensions of natural gas exports and that the export of crude oil will not exceed the level of imports for Canadian needs. To achieve these results would not require the construction of a Mackenzie Valley natural gas pipeline during this decade. This model would require the moderate development of eastern offshore gas and oil beginning in 1975; development of conventional oil and gas to continue at its present rate until 1975, after which time it would decline markedly; and limited oil sand development. Capital expenditure in the seventies to achieve this development case would be about $42 billion. This would require an 8.2 per cent annual growth rate in energy investment compared to the 10.7 per cent growth rate during the sixties.[18]

Case B, Standard Development, assumes that a Mackenzie Valley natural gas pipeline would be built beginning in 1975 with Mackenzie Delta gas reaching markets by 1978. In addition, eastern offshore gas and oil would be developed beginning in 1975. Conventional oil and gas development would continue at its present rate until 1975 and then would begin a gradual decline. Oil sand developments would proceed gradually. To achieve this result would require $50 billion in capital expenditures during the seventies. Expenditures would peak in 1976 and would then suddenly drop. The growth rate in energy investment for the decade would be 10.1 per cent. Case B is similar to *Case E, Delayed Development,* except that Case E would place the beginning of construction of the Mackenzie Valley natural gas pipeline in 1977 rather than in 1975.[19]

The other two cases, C and D, project still higher rates of development. *Case C, Extensive Development,* would add these extras to the Standard Development model: the construction of a Mackenzie Valley oil pipeline in 1978-79 and some pipeline construction offshore and from Ellesmere Island; offshore Arctic oil and natural gas development; and additional oil sands and refinery development. Ellesmere Island and Mackenzie Delta Oil would reach markets by the end of the decade. Case C would require capital expenditures of about $60 billion, involving a 13.5 per cent annual growth rate. *Case D, Maximum Development,* would add still further projects to those envisaged in Case C. These would include: the development of a uranium enrichment plant to begin in 1977; greater development of oil and natural gas production capacity on Ellesmere Island and in the Mackenzie Delta and offshore; oil sands development and expansion of refining capacity to proceed at maximum pace; further development on the east coast and in the Beaufort Sea and Arctic Islands by the end of the decade; and additional gas pipeline projects in the Arctic and the Beaufort Sea.[20] This model would call for capital expenditures of over $68 billion and would involve a 17.5 per cent annual growth rate during the 1970s.

The energy report foresees the possibility of a significant range of export levels for Canadian petroleum, depending on the development case adopted. In the early 1980s, Canada could be exporting as little as 800 thousand barrels of crude daily (to be equalled by offshore imports) if the Self-sufficiency model is adopted. The Standard Development model would involve exports in the early 1980s of 1.1 million barrels of crude daily. With Maximum Development crude exports could reach 2.8 million barrels daily.[21]

The possible range of natural gas exports would be even more affected by the choice of development model. The Self-sufficiency case would involve the continued export of .9 trillion cubic feet of natural gas per year, the amount already agreed to in previous undertakings. The Standard Development case would lead to an additional export of .8 trillion cubic feet of natural gas yearly. And if the gas plays in the high Arctic lead to pipeline development under the Maximum case, natural gas exports would skyrocket to 3.2 trillion cubic feet per year.[22]

While there will be considerable American pressure to gain the maximum crude oil imports from Canada, the pressure for natural gas, of which there is a greater U.S. shortage, will be even stronger.

The report concludes that the pipeline developments of the decade, foreseen in all of the cases except the Self-sufficiency case would involve large inflows of foreign capital and, in addition, large-scale imports of machinery and equipment.

The energy report was generally received by the Canadian public as no report at all, as a document which argued the pros and cons of every development model. In fact, the authors of the report deliberately set out to achieve this appearance. Some of the language used in the report makes this clear. For example, when discussing Canada's energy requirements the report talks of a standard forecast "based on a series of assumptions which represent a neutral or middle-of-the-road position."[23] In fact, there is nothing neutral at all in what the report does. The middle-of-the-road stance of the report consists in projecting the status quo forward. Its predictions are based on the following very real political assumptions: Canada's petroleum industry will continue to export a large proportion of its production to the U.S.; and the pace of development of Canada's energy industries will occur in response to continental and not Canadian patterns of demand.

The "Standard" Development model is made to appear as the moderate, non-political choice, which avoids the extremes of either the Self-Sufficiency or the Extensive and Maximum cases. In fact, the Standard case is nothing more than an attempt to push for the oil industry's number one current project, the Mackenzie Valley natural gas pipeline. The report's *short-run* political purpose can be seen from the fact that its major recommendation calls for the heaviest capital expenditures before 1976, or in other words, over a period of only three years. To put it more candidly, the report advocates the continuance of a continental energy policy for Canada. Its goal is to gain approval for projects that are now at the top of the oil industry's list. Later projects, outlined in the Extensive case and the Maximum case, can be taken care of in future reports.

As the makings of a continental energy policy have emerged, the Liberal government has varied its public posture according to the prevailing political climate in Canada. At various times, cabinet ministers have proclaimed their enthusiastic support for a continental energy policy; at other times they have hotly denied that such a policy exists. Sometimes, as is appropriate for the government of a dependent country, they fall back on the argument of *force majeur,* the argument that, after all, Canada can hardly be expected to differ with the United States on matters of fundamental importance.

But there is no doubt that a continentalist policy has been implemented. It has these major components: the development of Canada's petroleum industry according to an investment timetable dictated by the needs of the continental market rather than the Canadian market; an understanding on the part of the Canadian government that because whole industries and communities in the consuming country become dependent on imports of energy, exports of energy resources are long-term arrangements; and the realization by the Canadian government that any challenge to the American ownership of the Canadian petroleum industry would basically violate the continental energy policy.

Underwriting the continental energy policy is not a formally endorsed treaty but the reality of across-the-board American control of the Canadian economy. The policy is enforced by the fact that any significant violation of its fundamental features would invite massive economic retaliation by the United States in the manufacturing sector of the Canadian economy.

The continental energy policy is already fully in existence. Today the expectation is that the development of Canada's frontier oil and gas reserves in the Arctic and off the east coast, as well as the development of the oil sands in Alberta will take place in response to continental, rather than Canadian, energy demand.

Notes

[1]United States Information Service, *Canadian-American Relations, 1867-1967* (Ottawa, U.S. Information Service, 1967), v. 1, p. 44.

[2]*Ibid.*

[3]*Ibid.*, v. 1, p. 41.

[4]*Ibid.*, v. 1, p. 36.

[5]*Ibid.*, v. 1, pp. 38-39.

[6]*Globe and Mail,* June 23, 1970.

[7]James Laxer, *The Energy Poker Game* (Toronto, New Press, 1970) p. 1.

[8]U.S. Cabinet Task Force on Oil Import Controls report (the Shultz report), *The Oil Import Question, A Report on the Relationship of Oil Imports to the National Security* (Washington, D.C., U.S. Government Printing Office, 1970) p. 94.

[9]*Ibid.*, p. 335.

[10]Toronto *Star,* May 29, 1970.

[11]J.J. Greene, *Address to the Mid-Year Meeting of the Independent Petroleum Association of America,* Denver, Colorado, 1970, mimeographed by the Department of Energy, Mines and Resources, Ottawa, p. 19.

[12]*Ibid.*, p. 25.

[13]Laxer, *op cit.*, pp. 66-67.

[14]Canada, Department of Energy, Mines and Resources report, *An Energy Policy for Canada—Phase I* (Ottawa, Department of Energy, Mines and Resources, 1973), v. 1, p. 8.

[15]Toronto *Star,* September 28, 1970.

[16]*Globe and Mail,* January 8, 1973.

[17]*Oilweek,* October 15, 1973.

[18]Canada, Department of Energy Report, *op cit.*, v. 1, p. 210.

[19]*Ibid.*, v. 1, pp. 215-216.

[20]*Ibid.*, v. 1, p. 216.

[21]*Ibid.*

[22]*Ibid.*
[23]*Ibid.*, v. 1, p. 71.

9 The Federal-Provincial Energy Quagmire

The energy crisis did not threaten immediate shortages and rationing in Canada as it did in many other industrial nations. In this nation the energy crisis instead posed basic economic and political choices. The absence of a national industrial strategy and the integration of Canada into a continental economy underlay the incoherence of the political responses to the energy problem.

In mainstream Canadian politics, the energy issue predictably developed into a federal-provincial constitutional power struggle. The absence of coherent goals in national economic policy lent itself to confrontation between resource-producing and resource-consuming provinces, as well as to tests of strength between the federal and provincial governments.

The international oil price revolution of 1973 caused a complete realignment of Canadian regional political attitudes to oil. The old national oil policy had resulted in higher prices west of the Ottawa Valley, where Canadian crude oil supplied the market. East of the Ottawa Valley, cheaper overseas crude had meant cheaper fuel costs in Quebec and the Atlantic provinces. The sudden prospect that western Canadian oil would be cheaper than overseas oil gave the provincial governments in the producing provinces, Alberta and Saskatchewan, the bargaining power to opt for higher tax royalties and to press their view of how the nation's petroleum industry should be developed. After a decade of protecting Canadian crude from bootleg overseas oil slipped westward across the Ottawa Valley line, cheaper Canadian oil was desperately wanted east of the line.

The federal government's response to the sudden shift from a buyers' to a sellers' market in oil was to vacillate uncertainly between the perspectives of the producing and consuming provinces. The government remained committed to the complex of continental energy

83

policies developed over the previous decade, and it continued to promote continental development schemes for the future. For the federal government the issue was not one of determining the fundamentals of Canadian energy policy, questions such as who should own the country's resources and for which market should they be developed. The federal government's concern was over the extent to which it could maintain its jurisdiction over the evolution of the nation's energy policy.

In February 1973, the federal government asserted its jurisdiction over the movement of Canadian oil across provincial and international boundaries, by announcing crude oil export controls to begin on March 1, 1973.[1] This was a manoeuvre in Ottawa's developing struggle with the government of Alberta about where constitutional authority lay in the management of Canada's petroleum industry. The quotas actually set by the National Energy Board (NEB) were hardly restrictive. They allowed oil exports to continue at virtually the maximum capacity of the Interprovincial Pipeline system. The fact that oil exports grew by 18 per cent in 1973 reveals that the NEB was not acting because it was concerned greatly about tight supply of Canadian oil in relation to Canadian demand.

In mid-June 1973, concerned that mounting U.S. demand for Canadian petroleum products, such as gasoline and home heating fuels, could strain the capacity of Canadian refiners to meet the demand of the Canadian market, the federal government cut back on the export of refined products.[2]

The old national oil policy was scrapped in early September, 1973. In a brief statement to the House of Commons, Prime Minister Trudeau announced a series of policy initiatives on energy:

1) The oil industry will be asked to refrain from further price increases to Canadian consumers before January 30, 1974. This price restraint would apply except where, (to the satisfaction of the Minister of Energy, Mines and Resources) the increase in the cost of imported crude oil warrants a Canadian price increase;
2) The government intends to seek a control mechanism whereby higher prices in the U.S. market would not automatically increase prices at home in Canada. An export tax, or a national oil marketing board, are two possible control mechanisms. Discussions will be held as soon as possible with provinces and industry prior to the introduction of legislation.
3) The government will also hold early consultations with provinces and industry on the extension of pipeline facilities so as to enable Canadian oil to be shipped into Montreal. At a time of rapidly escalating international prices, this would put Canadian oil into competition with international oil, and would give additional

security against international disruptions of supply.[3]

The Prime Minister's announcement involved three significant energy moves: the price freeze on petroleum products; the export tax on oil (initially set at 40 cents a barrel to be collected by the federal government); and the scrapping of the national oil policy implied by the decision to build a pipeline to Montreal.

The Canadian government's initiative came at exactly the moment that the Nixon administration was declaring the objective of energy self-sufficiency for itself and was warning that the deteriorating Middle East situation could lead to oil boycotts by Arab countries. Much of the media coverage of the Prime Minister's announcement saw it as a Canadian declaration of independence from continental energy policies. This interpretation was incorrect. The fundamental decision to scrap the national oil policy was the necessary corollary to the new American energy strategy aimed at the eventual achievement of energy self-sufficiency for itself. As we have seen, the American Shultz report regarded the scrapping of Canada's national oil policy as the essential first step toward a fully harmonized continental energy policy. In September 1973, to his credit, Donald Macdonald, Canada's energy minister, reminded people of the fact that the Americans had wanted the pipeline to Montreal.[4]

The decision to substitute domestic oil in place of Canada's imports of overseas crude oil by the late 1970s is a basic decision that will affect future investment plans of the oil industry in this country. Many nationalists welcomed the decision. What they did not realize was that the pipeline decision fits into the larger framework of an emerging American strategy for continental self-sufficiency, not into the context of a disengagement of Canadian from American energy planning.

The truth of Canada's continuing commitment to a continental energy policy came home with brutal clarity only when the Middle East War and the subsequent Arab boycott forced Canada to line up unambiguously. On November 22, 1973, in a national television message to Canadians on the energy crisis, Prime Minister Trudeau addressed the problem in frankly continental terms. For him the underlying cause of the problem was the life style of the continent.

"Here in North America, with only 8 per cent of the world's population, our continent was using 38 per cent of the world's energy —putting tigers in our tanks, and new appliances in our homes, at an ever-increasing rate," he said.

The Prime Minister pledged to continue Canada's high rate of exports to the United States:

To many of you, it must seem odd that we should be sitting together tonight—talking about fuel shortages—worrying about soaring oil prices—while we continue to export half of our oil. That a country with enough energy resources to be reasonably self-sufficient should face shortages.

... Closely related to security and flexibility of our energy supplies is the question of our energy exports. I am deeply distressed—as I know many of you are—to hear charges that Canada has been "kicking the U.S. while it's down"—supposedly by reducing supplies, and increasing our prices, in order to profit from U.S. energy shortages.

These are the charges. Let's look at the facts. Far from reducing oil exports to the United States, Canada has been shipping to the U.S. more oil than ever before. Our projections for this year indicate we will ship to the U.S. 63 million barrels more oil than they purchased from us in 1972—an increase of 18 per cent. By increasing Canadian production, we have been able to respond to our neighbour's needs—while at the same time meeting our first responsibility, which is to ensure basic fuel requirements for Canadians. Consistent with that responsibility, the government's policy is—and will continue to be—to supply the U.S. from domestic oil production with all the help we possibly can. We are friends, and friends care about each other's problems.[5]

The Prime Minister also used this speech to explain why the old national oil policy had been scrapped by the government. He made it clear that the new policy would be conceived in terms of continental self-sufficiency to respond to petroleum demand on a continental basis. He stated:

... rapid changes of the seventies now demand new policies. The most important of these changes includes doubts about availability of oil from foreign suppliers, spectacular price increases for that oil, and soaring new energy demands by our chief oil customer, the U.S. This combination—of less security, higher prices and greater demand—has led to exciting new development possibilities for relatively costly and remote energy sources—such as those in the huge Alberta oil sands, the Arctic and the Atlantic Continental Shelf."

The Prime Minister concluded with the message the oil industry has been delivering to consumers in every capitalist country. "The days of cheap and abundant energy are over," he said.[6]

Perhaps though, the most penetrating statement on the Canadian political economy during these months came from Energy Minister Macdonald. He commented that Canada was not in a position to cut back its oil exports to the United States, because this would invite retaliation, perhaps in the form of the cancellation of the Canada-U.S. auto pact. Here was a virtual admission that the American domination of the Canadian economy and the existing extent of continental economic integration are the critical factors in determining what kind of oil policy Canada *can* have.

The federal government's other two initiatives, the price freeze and the export tax, were short-term steps taken to reinforce the fading popularity of the Trudeau government. The government's steps came at the same time as a Statistics Canada publication revealed that in August 1973, for the first time since World War II, the real incomes of Canadians actually fell due to the skyrocketing cost of living. The price freeze came at the end of a ten month period in which the oil industry had increased the price of crude oil by over 30 per cent (compared to an 8 per cent general price increase). In November 1972, the wellhead price of Canadian crude oil had stood at about $2.70; by September 1973, this had risen to about $3.70.

The export tax was necessitated by the price freeze. The export tax amounted to almost the difference between the frozen price of Canadian crude and the price of other imported crude in the Chicago market. The tax meant that the higher price for Canadian crude in the American market would increase federal government revenues rather than adding to the windfall profits of the oil industry. The export tax had no effect on the actual price of crude in the Chicago market. It simply meant that Canadian crude would sell in Chicago at the same price as other imported crude. The export tax was raised from 40 cents to $1.90 a barrel in December 1973, to $2.20 a barrel in January 1974 and to $6.40 a barrel for February and March 1974.[7]

The price freeze and the export tax were shrewd political steps for the Liberal government, because they did something in the short run for hard-pressed Canadian consumers.

But the price freeze and the export tax were temporary measures. At the time the new policy was announced in September 1973, Donald Macdonald conceded that there was "no way we can insulate Canadian consumers from all international market influences. The intention is to help even out the bumps to international marketing trends."[8]

Similarly, the Prime Minister stated in his television address on energy: "I do not regard the export tax as permanent."[9]

The pacing of federal government energy initiatives was, of course, influenced by the fact of a minority Liberal government. The de facto Liberal-NDP coalition government that has operated in Ottawa since the 1972 election came up with a series of energy policy steps in December 1973. In addition to extending the price freeze on petroleum products till the spring of 1974 (a move that would be popular with voters, especially in eastern Canada), Prime Minister Trudeau announced the immediate extension of the oil pipeline to Montreal and the final scrapping of the old national oil policy. The Prime Minister also announced plans to create a national petroleum company. The crown corporation would not operate in every phase of the petroleum industry in Canada. Rather, it would limit its activities to research and exploration work. With an initial projected budget of $40 million in the first five years of its existence, this crown corporation appeared designed to do little more than act as an appendage of the oil companies in their development operations. And since the projected national petroleum corporation would not itself be involved in the extraction, refining or marketing of petroleum products, it would do little more than lend a hand to the foreign-owned oil corporations in Canada.[10]

The response of the New Democratic Party to these developments was jubilant. Tommy Douglas, the party's energy critic, emerged from hearing Trudeau in the House, saying: "I think this is a turning point in the whole development of Canada's oil resources, and had we done this ten years ago we wouldn't be in the position we are today."[11]

When David Lewis, the federal NDP leader, heard Trudeau's position he was even more unstinting in his praise. "I can tell you now, on the basis of the fact that Mr. Trudeau has accepted our program, it is a total victory for the people of Canada and for NDP policies," Lewis said.[12]

Just what did this "total victory for the people of Canada" actually entail?

The Prime Minister had reiterated his position that before long, petroleum prices must be allowed to rise appreciably. As he put it:

> The days of abundant, cheap energy must come to an end. Canadians must be prepared to pay for additional costs (of exploration and development) or go without oil.
>
> We must, in the long run, allow prices to rise to a price high enough to allow development of the oil sands and other Canadian resources but not one bit higher.[13]

As we have seen, the government's energy report had indicated that such a policy meant an increase in the cost of oil to at least five dollars a barrel for Canadian crude (in constant 1972 dollars). The Prime Minister's statement meant that in the near future Canadians could look forward to steep increases in the price of petroleum, in the case of gasoline amounting to an initial six cents a gallon and later rising still further. For the oil companies, the future promised additional windfall profits.

And the NDP's reward for its long years of internal debate ending in rejected proposals for the nationalization of Canada's energy resource industries, was to preside over the creation of a national petroleum company whose budget could fall into the miscellaneous column of an Imperial Oil balance sheet and whose function would be to help fatten oil company profits.

The federal government's energy initiatives during 1973 did not upset the continental pattern on which the nation's petroleum industry had been based. They did, however, set in motion an important power struggle between the federal government and the province of Alberta, and to some extent Saskatchewan, about where power lay in the control of energy resources. Under the British North America Act, the provinces own the natural resources within their boundaries. The federal government, on the other hand, controls commerce involving interprovincial or international trade.

The issue of which level of government controls natural resources has been a bitterly fought question, which involves western Canada's hinterland economic status vis à vis central Canada. The inferior treatment of the West in its dealings with Ottawa on resources turned historically on the fact that the Prairie provinces did not gain control of their natural resources until 1930. Until then Prairie resources, unlike the resources in the other provinces, came under the jurisdiction of Ottawa.

The important historic struggle waged around the alienation of western resources gives the current battle between the province of Alberta and the federal government the aura of a populist crusade. But the chief crusader, Premier Peter Lougheed of Alberta, speaks for the corporate power of American oildom in Canada, not for the farmers of the West who formed the mass base in the pre-1930 struggle for Prairie control of natural resources. During 1973, Lougheed made skilful use of western sentiment in opposing the assertion of federal authority.

Lougheed termed excessive the federal government's action in establishing export controls in February 1973. He declared that the federal government underestimates the great potential of the Alberta oil sands. He stated:

We are in the position with this great reserve to meet the demand.
    It is not a desirable situation for Alberta to have this control under the National Energy Board. We have the capacity.
    What seems so difficult to get across to central Ontario is that Alberta crude belongs to the people of Alberta.[14]

The policy of the Lougheed government has been to alter the royalty system in the province and to increase the price of natural gas and crude oil so that the coffers of the provincial government and of the oil companies will benefit.

The provincial government, to increase its revenues, has adopted a plan which gives the oil companies the choice of paying a substantially higher tax on oil reserves or of paying royalties to the provincial government of 24.9 per cent for highly productive wells. The previous royalty was 16⅔ per cent.[15]

In an article in the *Canadian Forum,* Frank Roseman and Bruce W. Wilkinson examined the effects of the Alberta government's new tax system. Their article was written in the spring of 1973, when the price of crude oil had risen 93 cents a barrel in the years since 1962. They concluded that while Lougheed's new royalty and pricing system resulted in slight revenue gains for the province, it amounted to a veritable gold mine for the oil companies. As they describe the situation:

> We shall assume that the increased tax on oil reserves plus royalties will yield the equivalent of a 20 per cent royalty on all producing acres, both crown and freehold, regardless of the productivity of the oil wells. This percentage may be, on average, a trifle on the high side, but it is consistent with our objective of understanding, if anything, the loss to Albertans from present policies.
>
> But this royalty is not the net benefit to Albertans from the price increase. Albertans all have to pay the higher price for the oil bought for consumption within the province. Such consumption amounts to about 11 per cent of production of conventional crude. After adjusting for this fact, the *net* revenue to the province from an oil price hike is only 9 per cent of the price increase, not 20 per cent.
>
> Applying this reasoning to the $.93 per barrel price increases since 1962, and using the 1972 rate of production, we find that Alberta gets *$35 million* of the *incremental* revenues and the oil companies receive *$357 million.* In other words, the *loss to Albertans in one year* from failing to appropriate the economic rents to which they are entitled as the holders of the resources is $357 million.[16]

In their study Roseman and Wilkinson point out that, according to statistics of the Canadian Petroleum Association, costs of production declined by six cents a barrel between 1962 and 1972. In making their study though, they assumed only that prices had remained the same over the ten year period.[17]

While Lougheed is a master of the rhetoric of western discontent, his actions *aid* the oil companies in achieving truly majestic profit increases. For Lougheed the battle with the federal government was simply the convenient framework for his advocacy of the oil companies' desires with respect to price and development strategy.

When the federal government imposed its export tax on the sale of Canadian oil to the U.S., the Alberta Premier struck back with measures designed to rebuff this unwelcome federal intrusion. He called the federal policy "clearly detrimental" to Alberta, requiring from his province "strong responses", some of which might even be "unCanadian".[18]

The Premier's unbridled continentalism, his impatience at being confined in a Canadian context, was made clear in his statements. He was too easily prone to call Confederation into question, as when he said: "The imposition by the federal government of an oil export tax upon a province's natural resources is, in principle, contrary in our view to the spirit and intent of the essential terms of Confederation."[19]

Lougheed's strategy was to destroy the federal government's export tax by bringing in legislation allowing him the flexibility to establish higher provincial royalties on oil, based on the international price of oil rather than on the lower Canadian price. This would have the effect of forcing the Canadian price of oil up to the American price. Once this happened the federal export tax would be eliminated since it is based on the differential between the price of Canadian crude and the price of imported crude into the Chicago market.[20]

Lougheed's attempt to present himself as the champion of western discontent was highly transparent, as could be seen in his constant advocacy of the most pro-American position possible. He warned that the federal government controls had seriously damaged Canadian-U.S. petroleum relations and had jeopardized the prospects for a natural gas pipeline across the Canadian North.

In addition to his efforts to keep the federal government at bay, Premier Lougheed has been giving the green light to gigantic projects that would develop the Alberta oil sands under the control of foreign-owned oil companies and make the export of crude oil from this source possible. The Premier sees himself involved in a competition to develop the oil sands before the oil shales in Colorado can be developed. He believes he has four or five years lead time over oil shale development.[21]

In addition to the tensions between the federal government and the Alberta provincial government, the struggle over the future of Canada's petroleum industry has created a running battle between Lougheed's government and the government of Ontario.

Not surprisingly, the plans of the government of Alberta to raise natural gas and oil prices in response to new opportunity prices in the United States did not appeal to the government of the energy-deficit province of Ontario. As was the vogue, the provincial government of

Ontario produced an energy report of its own in December 1972, under the chairmanship of John J. Deutsch, the principal of Queen's University. The report concluded that the favourable energy environment of the past was ending for Ontario and that events external to Canada were responsible for this.

According to the Ontario report, "The effects of the rapid worldwide increase in the use of energy, and in particular, the effects of the energy crisis in the United States, will 'spill over' into Canada. This 'spill-over' has already begun and is having a pronounced effect on Canadian energy developments."[22]

It pointed with alarm to the increasing percentage of Canadian oil and gas production flowing to the United States and warned that this was leading to the depletion of Canada's conventional crude oil reserves and cheap supplies of natural gas. The result of this trend would be the peaking of Alberta's conventional crude production by the mid-seventies and future reliance on much more costly sources: that is, the oil sands, the Arctic and the Atlantic offshore area.

The Ontario report presented the problem in continental terms and reflected the battle going on between the major American oil companies and the great U.S. manufacturing corporations such as the auto companies and chemical companies. The Alberta-Ontario crisis was fought out by two governments representing different sets of multinational corporations: Alberta, the oil companies; Ontario, the branch plants of U.S. manufacturers, concerned about the cost of energy in their operations.

The report itself drew this analogy when it stated: "Ontario . . . finds itself in a rather unusual position of being one of North America's most energy intensive regions, and yet one of North America's most energy deficient regions—comparable in many ways to New York State."[23]

In arguing that Ontario should have first call on Alberta energy stores, ahead of American demand, the report made the point that during the sixties, when the Ontario market was limited to higher priced Alberta crude under the national oil policy, Ontario consumers had paid the higher price. Therefore, since Ontario had helped develop the Alberta petroleum industry at a cost to itself, it should not be penalized because of the change of market conditions in the seventies.

Throughout 1973 the Ontario government threatened to take the Alberta government to court to test the right of Alberta's Energy Resources Conservation Board to raise the price of natural gas for Ontario users. In reply, the Lougheed government warned that, if necessary, it would cut back the supply of natural gas to Ontario to safeguard its interests.[24]

At first glance it was easy (especially for residents of Ontario) to regard the position of the Ontario government as being in the national interest, opposed to the continentalism of the Alberta government. But Ontario's concern for cheap energy has always been a part of the province's strategy for enticing foreign manufacturers to set up branch plants. Ontario Hydro, owned by the province since 1905, has always seen its task as the provision of cheap power to industrialists. And in Ontario, manufacturing operations are mainly American-owned, just as is the case with resource-extractive industries in Alberta. Confederation has involved the creation of a region of secondary manufacturing in southern Ontario and Montreal that has as its hinterland the resource-extractive regions of the country. And in turn, this unequal Canadian system is simply a part of the larger imperial structure of American ownership of both manufacturing and resource-extractive industries in Canada. When Ontario speaks, it does not speak for the nation, but simply to safeguard its 50 per cent of Canada's total manufacturing output and its still higher proportion of branch plant manufacturing output.

The provincial governments of Alberta and Ontario are both locked into provincial regionalism. Often such a stance is justified to the people in terms of decentralization—the return of power to a level of government that is closer to the people. But the provincial regionalism rampant in Alberta and Ontario is actually a symptom of the balkanization of Canada and of continental integration. It has nothing to do with the high-sounding, but empty, talk of decentralization.

In December 1973, in a similar manifestation of regionalism, the government of Saskatchewan took action to ensure greater control over its oil industry. The Blakeney government introduced legislation giving it the power to take over oil rights held by companies on producing tracts. The bill would also give the province the power to set the wholesale price of oil and gas, create new taxes on wellhead prices and increase the acreage tax on oil companies to fifty cents an acre from the previous twenty cents.[25]

Saskatchewan, the nation's second largest petroleum-producing province, has about 15 per cent of the nation's proven reserves. Premier Blakeney expressed concern that Saskatchewan reserves have been falling for several years and at present rates of export (about 85 million barrels a year), the province's present reserves could run dry in 10 years. He announced it is his government's intention to control production in the province and to cut back output in order to guarantee cheap fuel for Saskatchewan.[26]

Saskatchewan, like Alberta, was challenging the federal government's export tax. Saskatchewan, under its plan, would establish a tax of its own amounting to 100 per cent of the difference between the wellhead price (to be set by the government) and world market prices. This would ensure that on oil exported from Saskatchewan the provincial government would control the tax room now occupied by the federal export tax.

The legislation, like that in Alberta, involved a constitutional question that could lead to important rulings in the Supreme Court, or even the disallowance of the provincial legislation by the federal government—a constitutional move the federal government had not made for 30 years. The Saskatchewan government's action came as an alternative to the nationalization of the province's oil industry, a measure that the provincial New Democratic Party had adopted as part of its programme in the fall of 1971. But in November 1973, the provincial NDP renounced nationalization of the oil industry at a convention in which the Premier himself intervened in the debate. However, pressure on the provincial government to undertake nationalization has continued. In December 1973, the Saskatchewan Federation of Labour called for an energy policy that would "use, preserve, protect and foster our resources for the people and remove their ownership and control from the hands of those who see them only from the grasping standpoint of huge profit gains to be secured without regard to human or national considerations."[27]

Following months of federal-provincial and inter-provincial wrangling, the federal-provincial energy conference of first ministers in January 1974 further demonstrated the disarray of Canadian federalism. The important event at the conference was Energy Minister Macdonald's presentation of a scheme for establishing a one-price system in Canada for crude oil. The Macdonald plan involved an increase in the wellhead price of Canadian crude oil from $4.00 to $6.00 a barrel. The two-dollar increase would be used to cushion the situation of eastern consumers dependent on imported crude and would also provide funds for further development of Canada's energy resources. Macdonald suggested the following breakdown of the revenues from the two-dollar increase: 48.8 per cent would go to subsidize eastern consumers; 28 per cent to the producing provinces; 16.6 per cent to the oil companies; and 6.6 per cent to the federal government. In the event the price rose an additional two dollars to $8.00 a barrel, Macdonald proposed the following breakdown of the additional revenues: 19.6 per cent to the producing provinces; 21.6 per cent to the oil companies; 16.0 per cent to the federal government; and 5.3 per cent to equalization (a government programme to offset regional economic disparities).[28]

Both directly and indirectly, the Macdonald plan would provide further windfall profits to the oil companies. Directly, they would get 16.6 per cent of the first two dollar a barrel increase and 21.6 per cent of the second two dollar a barrel increase. Indirectly, they would get much of the revenue that Macdonald earmarked as subsidies for eastern Canadian consumers. Since the same multi-national oil companies import crude oil into eastern Canada as produce it in western Canada, the subsidy to eastern consumers would simply fatten oil company profits even more, east of the Ottawa Valley line.

But the Macdonald plan failed to gain the acceptance of the premiers of the producing provinces. Alberta, Saskatchewan and Newfoundland (a would-be offshore producer), supported a strong provincial rights position at the conference. At the end of the two-day meeting, the first ministers emerged with a shaky and temporary scheme for a one-price system. The federal government was to subsidize eastern consumers through the revenues collected from the export tax on Canadian crude oil from February through April 1974.[29] During the period of respite a permanent formula for a one-price system was to be sought.

The premiers of the producing provinces returned home by no means prepared to accept a larger federal presence in the petroleum field. The Saskatchewan government promptly increased the price of its crude by $1.00 a barrel through the imposition of an additional provincial tax. Premier Lougheed of Alberta, back in Edmonton, announced that he would soon treble the provincial tax on natural gas, providing also for a higher take for the industry.[30]

At the federal level the Liberals appeared to benefit most from the jurisdictional war. They were in the happy position of having no Liberal provincial government in either oil-producing province and in being able to write the two provinces off federally. For the Conservatives, whose party divided into two wings, an Alberta wing and an eastern wing concerned about industrialists and individual consumers, the energy issue was a nightmare. The NDP was also forced to water down its already vague energy position, so that a conflict would not emerge between its federal caucus and the Saskatchewan provincial government. Behind closed doors in Toronto a few days before the federal-provincial energy conference, the NDP federal council retreated from its firm support for the oil price freeze and for the export tax.[31]

Mainstream politicans at both levels of government have responded to the energy issue by squabbling over who is to have jurisdiction in administering the nation's continental energy policy. Regardless of party label, they have failed to come to terms with the fundamental need to evolve a coherent national industrial strategy.

Notes

[1]Canada, Department of Energy, Mines and Resources report, *An Energy Policy for Canada—Phase I* (Ottawa, Department of Energy, Mines and Resources, 1973), v. 1, p. 8.

[2]*Wall Street Journal,* June 15, 1973.

[3]*Oilweek,* September 10, 1973.

[4]Toronto *Star,* September 15, 1973.

[5]Pierre Trudeau, *Notes for the Prime Minister's Statement on National TV, November 22, 1973* (Ottawa, Office of the Prime Minister, 1973).

[6]*Ibid.*

[7]*Globe and Mail,* January 4, 1974.

[8]*Oilweek,* September 10, 1973.

[9]Trudeau, *op. cit.*

[10]Toronto *Star,* December 7, 1973.

[11]*Globe and Mail,* December 7, 1973.

[12]*Ibid.*

[13]*Ibid.*

[14]Toronto *Star,* February 16, 1973.

[15]Frank Roseman and Bruce W. Wilkinson, "Who Benefits? The Alberta Energy Price Increases", *Canadian Forum,* June-July 1973.

[16]*Ibid.*

[17]*Ibid.*

[18]*Globe and Mail,* October 8, 1973.

[19]*Ibid.*

[20]*Financial Post,* November 13, 1973.

[21]*Ibid.*

[22]Report of the Advisory Committee on Energy to the Ontario government, *Energy in Ontario, the Outlook and Policy Implications* (Toronto, 1973), v. 1, p. i.

[23]*Ibid.,* v. 1, p. 25.

[24]*Globe and Mail,* November 11, 1973.

[25]*Globe and Mail,* December 22, 1973.

[26]*Globe and Mail,* December 5, 1973.

[27]*Globe and Mail,* December 20, 1973.

[28]Report presented at the Federal-Provincial First Ministers' Conference on Energy, *A presentation to provincial premiers of a suggested distribution of alternative prices of revenues on crude oil production,* January 22, 23, 1974 (Ottawa, Document No. FP-4134).

[29]*Globe and Mail,* January 24, 1973.

[30]*Globe and Mail,* February 11, 1973.

[31]*Globe and Mail,* January 21, 1973.

10 What's Next? The Mackenzie Valley Pipeline and the Alberta Oil Sands

Although not a work of great vision, this country's energy policy has not been without a centre of gravity. The oil companies have provided the direction and the statesmanship. And they are leading this nation along the continental energy path with a sureness of touch that is absent in the country's political leadership.

For the oil companies the future lies in gigantic projects that respond to continental rather than Canadian demand for energy. At the top of their list are two critical projects: the Mackenzie Valley natural gas pipeline and the development of the huge potential reserves of the Alberta oil sands.

First conceived in the late sixties, the Mackenzie Valley pipeline would bring natural gas from Alaska and the Canadian Arctic to southern Canada and the American Midwest. The main pipeline across Alaska and Canada would be 2500 miles in length. Its construction would cost about six billion dollars. Provided that government approval is obtained soon in Canada and the United States, the pipeline could be completed as early as 1978.

Several years of intense jockeying between two rival syndicates —the Northwest Project Study Group and the Gas Arctic System Study Group—each with its own scheme for the pipeline, eventually ended with the two groups merging under the name of Canadian Arctic Gas Study Ltd. To this merged syndicate were added Imperial Oil Ltd., Gulf Oil Canada Ltd., Shell Canada Ltd., and Canadian Pacific Investments Ltd. Add to that the Canada Development Corporation, controlled by the federal government, and the result is the most powerful array of corporate and state muscle ever put together on behalf of any project in this country's history.

In theory, the National Energy Board is the key body that must give the green light to a project like the Mackenzie Valley pipeline. In practice though, government ministers have shown their willingness to back the pipeline long in advance of the NEB hearings on the subject.

Several years ago, Prime Minister Trudeau described his vision of Mackenzie Valley development: "It is expensive, but so was the Canadian Pacific Railway a century ago. Is it too big a project for Canada? Only in the view of those who have lost faith in what Canada is all about."[1]

In March 1971, Jean Chretien, Minister of Indian Affairs and Northern Development, told an audience in Dallas, Texas: "We in Canada would welcome the building of such a gas pipeline through our country and would do everything reasonable to facilitate this particular development."[2]

Canada's Energy Minister, Donald Macdonald, has added his praise to that voiced by other cabinet ministers for the initiative being shown by the oil companies in moving into the North.

He has been attempting to convince the Americans that a Mackenzie Valley route entails great advantages for the United States in terms of national security. In May 1972, before the trans-Alaska pipeline system had been approved, Macdonald wrote a letter to U.S. Interior Secretary, Rogers Morton, which highlighted the security advantages of the Canadian route for Alaskan oil. (Presumably, the same arguments apply to gas.) Macdonald's letter stated:

> There would be many advantages arising from the use of a Canadian pipeline route. We believe it would enhance the energy security of your country by providing an overland route for your Alaska oil production, thereby servicing the oil deficit areas of the mid-continent and also the Pacific North West.
>
> Canada has an interest in the energy security of your country, and this land route for Alaska crude oil would enhance that security of supply to deficit areas in the United States. Furthermore, this security of supply could be further enhanced during the interim period of northern pipeline construction by extra Canada crude.[3]

No communication could demonstrate more clearly the continentalist stance of the Liberal government, willing to engage in the development of Canadian resources according to an American timetable. In this letter Macdonald is inviting the United States to regard Canada's resources as reliable reserves on which it can safely base its industrial and military planning. By stressing the security advantages for the U.S. in energy arrangements with Canada, he is entangling Canadian resource policy in the web of U.S. military planning—a sacrifice of Canadian sovereignty.

Not only have government ministers backed the pipeline prior to the NEB hearings on the subject, but a member of the consortium, Imperial

Oil Limited, has already made arrangements for the allocation of its Mackenzie Delta gas.

In 1972, Imperial arrived at sales agreements on Arctic gas with two companies in the United States, the Michigan-Wisconsin Pipe Line Company of Detroit and Chicago's Natural Gas Pipeline Company of America. These two pipeline companies agreed to lend Imperial ten million dollars a year, interest-free, for a period of four years that began in 1972. In return Imperial has given these companies first option to buy ten out of the initial twelve trillion cubic feet of natural gas discoveries on Imperial's Mackenzie Delta acreage. The pipeline companies, under the agreement, will lend an additional hundred million dollars to Imperial just before construction of the Mackenzie Valley pipeline is begun, and *another* hundred million dollars when the pipeline is completed. The magnitude of this deal can be appreciated from the fact that the amount of natural gas involved is considerably larger than the last sale of Canadian natural gas to the United States in September 1970, a two-billion-dollar sale of 6.3 trillion cubic feet of natural gas. Since Arctic gases will likely retail for between $1.00 and $1.25 per thousand cubic feet, Imperial's projected U.S. gas deal will thus lead to a retail sale price of between ten and twelve billion dollars.[4]

For consortium members like Imperial, the scheme has obvious merit. But convincing the public of that fact is the task of William Wilder, the chairman of the consortium. In an address to the Canadian Society for Corporate Growth, Wilder presented the case for the pipeline. He began with a brief dissertation on good and bad varieties of nationalism, the benefits of undertaking mutual projects with the United States, and the way in which his company is serving Canadian and U.S. interests. He stated:

It seems as though we Canadians have been worrying for more than a century about developing a sense of national pride and identity. Maybe we are trying too hard.

. . . I don't believe we need to shelter our nationalism in a cocoon to protect it from the rest of the world. It is not so fragile as some would have us believe.

Although negative nationalism is obviously bad, positive nationalism should be encouraged and nurtured. We need an attitude of enlightened self-interest, and we need to recognize the rest of the world. It is true that over the years there have been incidents where the best interests of Canada have not been served. However, they are minute compared to international dealings that have benefited this country.

I want to describe one specific example of how the interests of Canada and the U.S. can be served by recognition of mutual interests. The example involves my own company, and the transportation of natural gas from the Northwest Arctic.

This is the largest single project that private capital has ever tackled. It will embrace in the order of 5,000 miles of pipeline, much of it running below ground through some of the most difficult terrain on the continent. Of this, the Arctic Gas pipeline will embrace some 2,500 miles across Alaska and Canada to connect with other pipelines serving consumers in both Canada and the U.S.[5]

To date, he points out, the consortium has spent thirty-five million dollars in economic, engineering and environmental studies to prepare its case. Application will have to be made to government agencies in both the U.S. and Canada. In the U.S. the project will be examined by the Federal Power Commission, the Department of the Interior, and state agencies in Alaska and in the states which will receive the gas. In Canada the proposal will go to the National Energy Board, which will make a recommendation to the Cabinet, and to the Department of Indian Affairs and Northern Development, to obtain use of lands and a right-of-way across the Yukon and the Northwest Territories.

Wilder estimated that by the time the hearings are completed, the consortium will have spent more than seven years and sixty million dollars on the studies, hearings and pre-construction engineering. It is interesting to note that the preliminary expenditures undertaken to gain approval for this project exceed the expenses incurred in deciding who will form a government in Ottawa in a federal general election.

The consortium hopes to begin construction in the winter of 1976-77. Gas would begin flowing south from the Mackenzie Delta in 1978 and from the North Slope of Alaska in 1979.

Wilder asserts that the project will generate large earnings to Canadian investors who, he anticipates, will be the majority owners of the pipeline. Furthermore, substantial revenues will be realized from the export of natural gas as a result of the undertaking; government revenues will be enhanced and the Canadian economy will be broadly stimulated with resultant important employment gains.

In his address, Wilder warned that Canada's present reserves of natural gas would not fully satisfy Canadian needs beyond the end of this decade. Therefore, he suggested, the pipeline would give this country the benefits of economies of scale in extracting Arctic gas, because it is conceived in terms of American as well as Canadian markets.[6]

How convincing is Wilder's case?

As noted in an earlier chapter, the federal government's energy report placed Canada's remaining proven reserves of natural gas at 51.4 trillion cubic feet, more than enough to supply all of this country's needs and present export commitments to the end of the 1980s. Moreover, the report estimated (in the more conservative Estimate II of the Geological Survey of Canada), that an additional 30 trillion cubic feet of recoverable natural gas exists in the Canadian Prairies. This is more than enough to ensure Canadian needs into the 1990s at relatively low prices and to keep daily production up to required levels after the mid-1980s, when output from present sources begins to slow down due to falling natural gas pressures.[7]

In light of this it is difficult to interpret Wilder's warning about Canadian natural gas reserves as anything other than a display of the petroleum industry's current practice of underestimating Canadian reserves to frighten the public into going along with projects that actually only make sense in terms of American demand.

To some extent Wilder hinted at this when he said, "The one point that remains clear is the need for a pipeline that transports both Canadian and U.S. gas. It is extremely difficult to envision how markets in Southern Canada could be served at a reasonable price with Mackenzie Delta gas without the economies of scale provided by the much larger U.S. market demand."[8]

With this point we can, of course, readily agree. Since there is no shortage of natural gas in Canada, the market for new gas brought from distant northern sources and priced at three times the price of our available supplies would indeed be limited.

What about the economic effects of building the pipeline?

Since the project is not needed in terms of Canadian demand for natural gas, the problem is that if Canadian capital is mobilized for the pipeline, it will make capital scarce for all other economic development. This means forgoing the development of manufacturing industries that would provide many more jobs in the country.

Of course, this problem can be solved by using foreign capital. But if huge amounts of foreign capital are imported into Canada for the pipeline (not to mention the even more costly James Bay Hydro development in Quebec proceeding at the same time), the increased demand for Canadian currency will drive up the value of the Canadian dollar. This in turn will hurt Canada's exports across the board. (If the Canadian dollar is valued at $1.10 American, it takes more American dollars to buy a dollar's worth of Canadian goods. This amounts to a self-imposed hurdle for our exports.)

A California economist, concerned about the U.S. balance of payments, has estimated the trade effects of an upward revaluation of the Canadian dollar: a 5 per cent increase would result in a $715-million negative trade shift for Canada with the U.S., resulting from decreased exports and increased imports; a 10 per cent increase would result in a $1.6 billion negative trade shift.[9]

There is, of course, one way around the problem. If the foreign capital raised for the project is simply spent abroad on equipment for the project, it will not affect the Canadian exchange rate. But then, neither will it create any jobs in Canada. On the other hand, if spending is done in Canada, jobs in secondary manufacturing would be destroyed (as the higher value of the Canadian dollar would hurt exports from more labour-intensive industries).

Ironically, the Americans may well prefer to have the bulk of the capital for the pipeline raised in Canada, and they may well prefer Canadian control of the whole venture. This way, the very heavy cost of construction would fall on Canadians, who would then earn a low fixed rate of return on the pipeline, which as a common carrier, would be treated like a public utility. Meanwhile, the real profits would be made by the petroleum companies whose gas would flow through the pipe to market.

The federal government was understandably upset when, in the spring of 1973, a document prepared by the Department of Finance the previous fall, but not released, was leaked to the public. The document did not paint a rosy picture of the economic impact of the pipeline on Canada. It pointed to the inflationary effects which would be exerted by the pipeline, and predicted that upward pressures on the value of the Canadian dollar would result from the importation of American capital.

The document concluded that only 150 to 200 permanent jobs would result from the Mackenzie Valley pipeline. Furthermore, it estimated that under existing tax regulations, returns to the federal treasury would be minimal (only $73 million a year following a government expenditure of $200 million). Finally, it forecast "a potentially serious upward pressure on the level of Canadian energy prices."

The document's position was summarized in the statement that "the construction and operation of a northern gas pipeline, even if it were to carry a substantial proportion of Canadian gas, would likely prove to be a mixed blessing to Canada."[10]

What about the effects on the people of the North? On his return from a tour of the Arctic, economist Mel Watkins wrote:

Exploring for oil and gas and bringing it to wellhead creates some jobs, but on a one-shot basis. If direct employment is small in general, it is even less for the native people and mainly in low-paying manual jobs. For instance, during the construction of the Pointed Mountain Pipeline, only thirty native people were employed for a maximum of three months, while three hundred twenty workers were brought in from the South. In 1970, after the federal government had invested $9 million in Panarctic, it had employed only six natives at $1.75 an hour.

The results of this are profound. While the majority of the population in the Northwest Territories is still native people the pattern is quickly changing, particularly in the Mackenzie Delta where the biggest oil and gas play is taking place. Ten years ago, the town of Inuvik had 1,000 native inhabitants; today, there is a population of 3,000 and the majority is white. Furthermore, the whites live in modern, subsidized housing, the natives in slum conditions. What begins as an employment effect ends up creating a segregated town and racial discrimination. The losers just happen to be the original people, those who are, in lawyer Peter Cumming's moving phrase, "truly of the very land they occupy". The multi-national corporation and the Canadian state have become invaders, creating a pattern of oppression that we like to imagine is found only in Third World colonies.[11]

The Mackenzie Valley pipeline is the most important currently proposed physical manifestation of Canada's continental energy policies. Its completion will tie this nation even more closely to the economic and political control of the United States.

In his crucial energy statement to the House of Commons in December 1973, Prime Minister Trudeau committed the government to actively support the building of the Mackenzie Valley pipeline. The statement was a part of the package endorsed by the NDP in the confidence vote that followed. While David Lewis crowed about "total victory for the people of Canada," the pipeline project was taking another step toward final approval. David Lewis, the de facto cabinet minister, had made his small contribution to the further colonization of his country, a contribution which entailed reversing the long-standing NDP opposition to the pipeline.

Ironically, the only dark cloud on the horizon of Canadian Arctic Gas Study Ltd. was not the NDP's balance of power position in the House of Commons, but the possibility that a rival project would undercut it. The challenge came in the form of a proposal by the El Paso Natural Gas Company of Houston, Texas, to liquify the Arctic gas and transport it by tanker from Alaska to west coast American ports. El Paso claims its scheme can deliver the gas to market more cheaply than the Mackenzie Valley pipeline can. If the El Paso scheme gets the nod from the Americans though, it won't mean the end of pressures to export Canadian Arctic gas. El Paso has made it clear that it would gladly build a pipeline from the Mackenzie Delta to Alaska, from where the Canadian gas could be shipped to U.S. markets.[12] The threat of the rival El Paso scheme is now being used by officials of the

Mackenzie Valley pipeline consortium to warn the Canadian government that any efforts it makes to increase the benefits to the public from the pipeline could result in the loss of the project to El Paso. The outcome of the battle between the Canadian Arctic Gas Study consortium and El Paso will only determine which side garners the commercial advantage of having its project approved. Either way the United States can hardly lose.

While the Mackenzie Valley pipeline is the key to increasing future exports of Canadian natural gas, oil exports depend on the rapid development of the Alberta oil sands. The oil sands contain reserves that are thirty times as large as Canada's total present proven reserves of conventional oil.

In September 1973, Alberta Premier Lougheed went on local television to announce to the province that Syncrude Canada Ltd. had signed an agreement to proceed with a billion-dollar oil sands development project. The site for the project would be in northeastern Alberta, twenty-eight miles north of Fort McMurray, and would involve extraction and processing on its 50,000 acres.[13]

Backing the project is Syncrude Canada Ltd., a consortium of American-owned oil companies. Imperial, Cities Service Athabasca, Inc., and the Atlantic Richfield Company each have a 30 per cent interest and Gulf Oil Canada Ltd. holds the remaining 10 per cent.[14] Managing contractor for the project will be another American firm, Bechtel Ltd., which is carrying out the same function in the James Bay hydro-development project in Quebec.

According to Syncrude president F.K. Spragins, who came to Canada from Texas in 1942 to work for Imperial Oil, production should begin in 1978. The capacity of the operation, to be reached after several years of production, will be 125,000 barrels a day of synthetic crude oil.[15]

Under the agreement reached between the Alberta government and Syncrude, the province is to get 50 per cent of the profits from the venture, but would be guaranteed a seven and a half per cent royalty on sales after five years of production should profits drop below the equivalent return.

Lougheed also announced the creation of a crown corporation, the Alberta Energy Company, in which the public will be able to buy fifty per cent of the shares. This corporation will have an option to buy 20 per cent of the Syncrude operation when it goes into production.[16]

The problem with this system of guaranteeing a return to the public is that the president of Syncrude says he does not expect the operation to declare any profits for the first seven years of operation. Furthermore, the company intends to write off its payments to the Alberta government as expenses deductable from its payment of federal corporation taxes. Public participation in the project may well turn out to be mere window dressing, with almost no returns going to the provincial treasury or federal coffers.

The Alberta government is going full steam ahead with the development of the Alberta oil sands in spite of advice it received from eighty senior civil servants in a confidential report submitted in August 1972. The report made it clear that pressures to develop the oil sands did not arise from Canadian demand. To the contrary, it stated:

> Alberta is not under any pressure to develop synthetic crude oil from the bituminous tar sands for the purpose of meeting either Albertan or Canadian petroleum requirements. The pressure to develop synthetic crude from the tar sands emanates from markets external to Canada. . . .[17]

The Syncrude project is seen by Alberta oilmen as a giant pilot project, to be followed quickly by more and larger ventures. (But Syncrude is, in fact, the second, not the first, oil sands project. Back in 1968, Great Canadian Oil Sands Ltd., a subsidiary of the Sun Oil Co. of Philadelphia, began to develop a pilot oil-sands operation. By the end of 1972, the development's daily oil production totalled 50,900 barrels. At this level of output, it had already become one of the biggest strip mining operations in the world, moving close to 200,000 tons of material daily.[18]) Not far behind the launching of the Syncrude development was a bid from Shell Canada Ltd. to undertake its own billion-dollar oil sands project. Slated to begin production in 1980, the development plans call for the project to achieve full production two years later of 100,000 barrels a day. The Shell lease area, which is nearly 50,000 acres in extent, contains vast reserves: 3,280 million barrels of recoverable bitumen—enough to sustain the desired output for about 65 years.[19]

Oil company executives like to talk of the oil sands as "Canada's Middle East". In a speech to an institutional investors' conference in Montreal in November 1973, Jack C. Threet, vice-president of Shell Canada Ltd., said he could foresee his company operating *thirty* heavy-oil and oil-sands plants by the year 2000.[20]

Furthermore, oilmen are telling the Canadian public that oil sands development is a must if Canada is to extend the Interprovincial pipeline east to Montreal and supply the market east of the Ottawa Valley with Canadian oil.

In a speech to the Calgary Chamber of Commerce in December 1973, Syncrude President F.K. Spragins said, "Even if we were to contemplate a pipeline to Montreal tomorrow and to fill it with all possible production from Alberta, we would still, in a very few years, be in the position of not being able to supply all of Eastern Canada's needs."[21] Spragins claimed that the primary purpose of oil sands development was to meet Canadian needs. But, significantly, he stated that this did not exclude the possibility of exports.[22]

In November 1973, Herman Kahn appeared before the Canadian Cabinet like a corpulent apparition from an Ian Fleming novel to present his plan for the development of the oil sands. Kahn, who spends his time at the Hudson Institute, a think-tank in New York State, has devoted much of his life to working out a strategic overview of the military escalation stages that lead to nuclear war.

In recent years Kahn has turned his mind to the problems of economic development in countries dependent on the United States. Some of his recent exploits have included sending a "flying think-tank" over Angola (for airborne brainstorming sessions, the object of which was to provide the Portugese government with an economic strategy to bolster its colonial regime), and convincing the government of Colombia to reroute that country's waterways. At present, he is trying to convince the government of Brazil to redevelop the Amazon river as a "Great Lakes of South America".[23]

Kahn used a slide show to present his ideas on the oil sands to Canadian cabinet ministers. He told the ministers that Canada should import 20 billion dollars in development capital from Japan, the United States and western Europe to allow for the speedy international development of the oil sands as a source of massive crude oil exports to the major industrial nations. He foresees the need to import machinery and equipment into Canada on a gigantic scale to carry out the project. And, borrowing a leaf from the CPR, which used Chinese labourers to build the trans-continental railroad, Kahn envisages the work on the oil sands being done by migrant South Korean workers.[24]

One federal cabinet minister, at least, appears to have been mesmerized by Kahn's performance. In a speech at the University of British Columbia on February 7, 1974, Supply Minister Jean Pierre Goyer advocated the rapid development of just such a project.[25] Even if such extreme fantasies belong in the corridors of the Hudson Institute's imagination, the drive to develop the oil sands for export, particularly to the United States, should not be discounted.

The massive projects now on the agenda of the Canadian oil industry depend for their realization much more on the determined planning of the oil companies than on the fitful behaviour of the politicians. Behind the projects is a very real corporate government with its own internal political leadership. And the man at the centre of that leadership is W.O. Twaits, chairman and chief executive officer of Imperial Oil.

Twaits casts himself in the role of a kind of secular priest surrounded by idiot government bureaucrats. He talks as though developing Canada's oil industry is a heavy and thankless task, constantly made harder by interfering nincompoops. He invariably gives the impression that the oil industry has had such a bad time of it in this country that the very next royalty increase, extension of the export tax, or price freeze will lead the oilmen to pack their bags and head off to some more promising banana republic.

But Twaits is also a man of patience, and he knows how to play the percentages. His rule of thumb is time-honoured in the oil industry —always complain no matter what action the government takes, and always sound as though you were drastically short of investment capital no matter what your level of profits is.

During the energy crisis Twaits has tirelessly promoted his objectives—the development of the oil sands, the building of the Mackenzie Valley pipeline and the continued development of Canada's energy resources according to continental and not Canadian needs. He has not gotten everything he wanted. He has had to put up with the export tax and the price freeze. But he has been assured by the federal government that these are temporary measures. And, much more important, the federal and the provincial governments have come around to his point of view on the oil sands and the Arctic. He has seen the emergence of a basic consensus among the nation's three major parties on the continued development of Canada's petroleum industry under American corporate ownership, with its priorities established by American demand patterns.

On the continental nature of Canada's energy policy, Twaits said in the spring of 1973: "It is as foolish to suggest that these two countries [Canada and the U.S.] can follow unrelated or uncoordinated energy policies as it is to suggest that the countries of western Europe, which are interlinked in similar ways, can proceed separately in matters of energy."[26]

On the need to see the nation's northern petroleum development in continental and not simply Canadian terms, Twaits affirmed that "it would not be economic to explore at all if we were looking at Canadian demand only."[27]

On one occasion, when Walter Gordon suggested public development of the nation's northern resources, Twaits replied, "It sounds like Walter's old idea of buying back Canada, which doesn't make economic sense to me. Why does he think government would run it [northern exploration] better than industry?"

"I still hold the peculiar notion that it's better to risk private money—because it's still a horserace—than to risk public revenues," Twaits explained.[28]

The Imperial chairman cautioned of the danger of the development of northern petroleum reserves being held up by pesky government hearings. "I would hate to see this getting into the horrible situation Alaska is in. That's just a waste of money and talent," he said, shrugging off the whole area of protecting the environment.[29]

When Imperial's 1973 profits were announced, revealing a 49 per cent increase over 1972, Twaits was still in there pitching. He declared that he was not satisfied with the higher level of profits, and warned: "If we have to invest at three times the rate, we have to get three times the returns."[30]

Notes

[1]James Laxer, "Scenario for a sell-out", *Last Post,* March 1973.

[2]*Ibid.*

[3]*Ibid.*

[4]Data card on Imperial Oil Ltd., August 10, 1973, compiled by the Financial Post Corporation Service, Toronto.

[5]*Financial Post,* October 27, 1973.

[6]*Ibid.*

[7]Canada, Department of Energy, Mines and Resources report, *An Energy Policy for Canada—Phase I* (Ottawa, Department of Energy, Mines and Resources, 1973), v. 1, p. 89.

[8]*Financial Post,* October 27, 1973.

[9]James Laxer, "Canadian Manufacturing and U.S. Trade Policy", in Robert Laxer, ed., *(Canada) Ltd.* (Toronto, McClelland and Stewart, 1973) p. 145.

[10]Federal Department of Finance position paper, published by the *Canadian Forum,* under the title, "The Export Rip-off: the Civil Service Report", June-July 1973.

[11]Mel Watkins, "Resources and Underdevelopment", in Robert Laxer, ed., *(Canada) Ltd.* (Toronto, McClelland and Stewart, 1973) p. 122.

[12]*Financial Post,* November 30, 1973.

[13]J.C. Russell, "Syncrude and Peter Lougheed: Giving it all Away", *Canadian Forum,* January 1974.

[14]Data card for Imperial Oil Ltd., December 5, 1973, compiled by the Financial Post Corporation Service, Toronto.

[15]*Oilweek,* September 24, 1973.

[16]Russell, *loc. cit.*

[17]*Ibid.*

[18]*Financial Post,* June 23, 1973.

[19]*Oilweek,* September 10, 1973.

[20]*Oilweek,* December 3, 1973.

[21]*Globe and Mail,* December 8, 1973.

[22]*Ibid.*

[23]Paul Dickson, *Think Tanks* (New York, Ballantine Books, 1971) pp. 100-107.

[24]Reported by W-5, CTV network show, February 17, 1974.

[25]Toronto *Star,* February 8, 1974.

[26]Toronto *Star,* March 6, 1973.

[27]*Oilweek,* April 9, 1973.

[28]*Financial Post,* July 28, 1973.

[29]*Ibid.*

[30]*Financial Times,* February 18, 1974.

11   Energy Policy and Canadian Industry

The most puzzling thing about Canada's continental energy policies is why they are allowed to persist.

Why are they continued when they are so obviously in the American and not in the Canadian interest? Why do Canadian governments allow American corporations to export half of Canada's petroleum and capture most of the profits from the nation's petroleum industry? Why do they allow a continental demand pattern to set the pace of Canadian energy development, when it is so clear that such a policy will quickly increase energy prices for Canadians? Why do they tax American-owned petroleum companies at the lowest level of any corporation in Canada, when these companies provide so few jobs for Canadians?

The first response to such questions might be to search for Canadian politicians in the pay of the oil companies. While undoubtedly such cases exist, they do not, in themselves, explain very much. Corrupt politicians and oil company contributions to political campaign funds help to grease the wheels on a day-to-day basis. But they do not adequately account for a situation in which the nation's entire development strategy can be distorted over a very long period of time.

Neither do matters of political preference, such as the Liberal Party's avowal of continentalism since the 1880s, explain the government's behaviour. The continentalism of the Liberal Party is also more a symptom than a cause.

Canada's continental energy policy can only be explained as *an aspect* of American corporate and state control of *the entire Canadian economy*. Only such an approach reveals fully the place of Canada's continental energy policy in a continental economic system.

For Canada, a continental energy policy is an integral part of a branch plant industrial strategy. Canadians are often told that in a country so diverse regionally it is natural that some regions export resources while others specialize in manufacturing. Therefore, this reasoning goes, a national resource and industrial strategy necessitates trade-offs to satisfy diverse regional needs.

But rather than accepting the disintegration of Canada's national economy as a natural phenomenon, it should be understood as the logical outcome of the peculiar nature of Canadian business. Canadian capitalists have always specialized in serving as commercial middlemen in someone else's empire. Canadian merchants and bankers have profited from the volume of domestic economic activity generated by the ventures of foreign firms in Canadian resource and manufacturing industries.

Canada's commodity production, in both resource and manufacturing sectors, has been increasingly organized within the framework of branch plant corporations. Branch plant corporations control primary production in the nation's mineral and forest industries as well as key areas of manufacturing such as transportation equipment, electrical products, machinery, chemicals, rubber and plastics, and petroleum products.

Since World War II, foreign corporations in resource extraction and in manufacturing have become so dominant in Canada they have replaced Canada's native trading and banking businessmen as the decisive consideration in establishing Canada's economic policies. Foreign corporations manage the Canadian economy and the Canadian state in their own interest, and distort and confine Canadian development within a framework that is most profitable to them.

The informal American control of the Canadian state can be demonstrated in numerous ways for the period since World War II. One sure indicator of American power is the fact the large U.S. multi-national corporations pay the lowest taxes of any corporations in Canada.

The ultimate determinant of authority in any state reposes in the apparatus of physical coercion—the military. The nature of the Canadian-American military "alliance" ensures American control of Canada in this final sense. The vast inequality in power between the two countries ensures that the "alliance" is little more than a formal guarantee that Canada is part of the American empire. American control is also exercised in an immediate sense, because the U.S. military enjoys direct command over important sections of Canada's NORAD (North American Air Defence) forces and is involved in the training of large numbers of Canadian military personnel.

In the 1950s, Canadian parliamentarians were, on occasion, barred from parts of the Canadian North that were open to U.S. military personnel. During the Cuban missile crisis in 1962, NORAD heaquarters in Colorado demonstrated its power to put Canadian forces on alert before the Canadian government had assented to this. Again, in the fall of 1973, when President Nixon placed U.S. forces on alert (more to control impeachment-hungry U.S. congressmen than to counter any Soviet threat), the Canadian forces in the integrated sections of NORAD went on alert. Canadian government denials of this were somewhat pathetic in the face of public confirmation by Canadian military personnel in NORAD's Colorado headquarters.

American corporations value Canada primarily as a resource base and consumer market. Canada's economic history since World War II has evolved as a function of this; the rhythm of Canadian development has been in response to the economic fortunes of the American empire.

During the decades of clear U.S. hegemony in the capitalist world, from 1945 to the mid-1960s, American investment poured into Canadian resource and manufacturing industries. It was the U.S. need for Canadian resources that established this country's strategic importance in the American empire.

The era of American world power was also to be an era of growing American dependence on raw materials from many countries. Since 1900, the United States has gradually shifted from being a net exporter to a net importer of raw materials. By the mid-fifties, the United States was importing over half of its required metals. Even earlier, the Korean war had made the Americans acutely aware of their reliance on resources from many countries for strategic purposes.

The need for access to resources was presented to the American people as part of the world-wide anti-communist crusade. In 1952, the report of President Truman's Materials Policy Commission was published under the title *Resources for Freedom*. Known as the Paley report, the study advocated a systematic attempt to enhance American access to the resources of U.S. allies and satellites the world over. U.S. investment in resource-rich countries would be followed by the dependence of those countries on U.S. manufacturing—all to the benefit of American business and American security.

The Paley report summed up U.S. objectives as follows: "The over-all objective of a national Materials Policy for the United States should be to ensure an adequate and dependable flow of materials at the lowest cost consistent with national security and with the welfare of friendly nations."[1]

Since World War II the export of Canadian primary products to the United States has grown steadily. Rather than becoming more diversified, over the past two decades Canadian trade has become more narrowly centered on the United States. Between 1950 and 1970, the proportion of Canadian exports destined for the American market increased from 60 to 68 per cent, and the proportion of Canadian imports from the U.S. increased from 67 to 71 per cent.[2]

In recent years, Canadian mineral production has grown at an annual rate of 11 per cent. An article prepared by the Mineral Resources Branch of the Department of Energy, Mines and Resources for the *1972 Canada Year Book,* pointed to the role of resource exports in the Canadian economy:

> The great size of Canada's mineral industry is based largely upon export sales. Apparent domestic minerals consumption is equivalent to proportions of mineral output ranging from 6 per cent for potash and nickel to about 20 per cent for iron ore and about 43 per cent for copper. The value of minerals and fabricated minerals exported in 1970 was 90 per cent of mineral production value.
>
> Exports of minerals and fabricated mineral products have led several great and sustained booms in the Canadian economy in the past and they have been a major factor in the surge in recent Canadian export trade.[3]

There is a clear link between Canada's role as an exporter of raw materials and semi-fabricated products to the United States and the underdeveloped state of this country's manufacturing. Canada has been a net importer of most types of manufactured goods and has been paying for these with net exports in petroleum, pulp and paper, minerals, primary metals, lumber, wheat and whiskey. In 1970, Canada had a two and a half billion dollar deficit in its trade in manufactured goods.[4]

Canadians are by far the world's leading importers of manufactured goods, importing 463 dollars' worth per capita per year in 1969 (as compared with $239 per capita per year in the European Common Market, $116 per capita per year in the United States and $41 per capita per year in Japan).[5] Imports of manufactured goods in 1970 amounted to nearly 20 per cent of the final value of the manufactured goods produced in Canada; in the United States imports of manufactured goods amounted to only 4 per cent of the final value of goods manufactured in the U.S. Significantly, the 4 per cent figure in the United States was regarded as so high that it merited government measures to protect American manufacturing. In sharp contrast, Canadian governments had not regarded an invasion of the domestic manufacturing market nearly five times greater as serious enough to warrant a coherent industrial strategy.

Canada has been left behind in major high-technology industries that have been growing rapidly in the industrialized countries over the past ten years. The country has been running up increasing trade deficits; this is especially true of the plastics industry, pharmaceutical products, scientific instruments and electronic computers.[6]

Ironically, because of Canada's failure to develop a science-intensive manufacturing sector, the country is often a net importer of a finished product based on minerals that Canada leads the world in extracting. In spite of the nation's net exports of oil and natural gas, Canada is a net importer of petrochemicals. Canada is the world's largest producer of nickel and asbestos, but a net importer of manufactured nickel and asbestos products. The country imports much of its fine paper, in spite of its position as the world's leading exporter of pulp and paper. The world's second largest producer of aluminum, Canada nonetheless imports it in its more sophisticated forms.

Canada's pre-eminence as an exporter of raw materials is the obverse of its weak manufacturing base.

A striking feature of Canadian manufacturing is the relatively small percentage of the country's work force it employs. In 1965, only 24.5 per cent of the paid non-agricultural work force in Canada was employed in manufacturing. By 1971, the percentage had dropped to 21.3 per cent.[7]

Among western countries, only Greece and Ireland have a lower percentage of their work force employed in manufacturing. For the United States, the comparable figures are these: in 1965, 29.7 per cent of the paid non-agricultural work force was employed in manufacturing; in 1971, 26.3 per cent.[8] The disparity in proportions of the work force employed in manufacturing in Canada and the United States is not, of course, accounted for through greater Canadian productivity. In 1970, while Canadian manufacturing activity accounted for $20 billion in value added, U.S. manufacturing activity accounted for $300 billion in value added.[9] Adjusting for the fact that the U.S. population is about ten times the Canadian, this represents a U.S. superiority of 3 to 2 in terms of the size of the two economies.

But differences between a resource-based hinterland economy and the economy of a metropolitan country are qualitative as well as quantitative. Durable goods production, for example, the strategic centre of any industrial economy, is the final result of the labours of less than half the manufacturing workers in Canada; in the U.S. 60 per cent of manufacturing workers are involved in the production of durable goods.[10]

The disparity between the two economies becomes clear when we examine manufacturing sector by sector. Canada has relatively greater manufacturing employment than the U.S. in only three categories: food and beverages, tobacco products, and wood products. In all other categories there is relatively greater U.S. employment. This is especially true in high-technology industries such as machinery, electrical products, chemicals and scientific and professional equipment.[11]

At the very centre of Canada's manufacturing weakness is the state of machinery production in this country. It is this sphere of production that makes possible production in all the other categories of manufacturing. In 1971, there were 72,800 workers employed in this field in Canada and the value added in the industry was just over seven hundred million dollars. In the U.S. there were 1,791,000 workers employed in machinery production and value added totalled over $31.5 billion. Therefore, while U.S. relative employment was two-and-a-half to one compared with Canada's, the relative U.S. superiority in output amounted to four-and-a-half to one. In 1970, Canada imported $1,783,268,000 worth of machinery, more than the total value of machinery produced in Canada, and of this amount, $1,421,809,000 was imported from the United States.[12]

The decisive weakness of Canadian machinery production guarantees Canadian compliance with overall U.S. economic objectives. Any Canadian political decision to substitute Canadian for American priorities in the development of this country's resources would lead to U.S. retaliation in the sphere of machinery production. Any interruption of the flow of American-produced machinery into Canada would create chaos in the Canadian economy.

Canadian politicians know that their power is limited to squabbling about which level of government is to preside over the nation's continentalist resource policies. At the federal-provincial conference on energy in January 1974, much was said about provincial or federal control of resources and about equalization formulas, but little was said about who owns the oil industry and the effect of exporting half of this country's oil and gas to the United States.

Qualitatively, Canada's economy is much weaker today than at any time in this century. The era of complete American control, which began with World War II, has progressively undermined this country's capacity to produce commodities independently. In addition to the American stranglehold on the supply of machinery for Canadian industry, the growing dependence of this country on imported technology weakens its capacity for independent action.

A 1972 background study for the Science Council of Canada demonstrated the link between branch plant manufacturing in Canada and the low level of technological innovation in the Canadian economy. In spite of spending relatively high amounts per capita on education, Canada has a dismal record in technological innovation, in comparison with other developed countries. This is because branch plant manufacturers normally import technology from their parent companies in the United States rather than develop it here. This does not merely affect end-product (finished product) manufacturing. Parts and components for end-product manufacturers are usually designed according to specifications also developed by the parent company. Companies engaged in end-product manufacturing and companies producing parts and components often establish jointly sponsored research communities for the purpose of product innovation. This process cannot develop in a branch plant economy where would-be local suppliers have to compete with foreign firms that have several years' lead time in producing parts and components for new end-products.[13]

In the 1960s, the federal government attempted to promote research and development in Canadian industry through a policy of generous tax incentives. Many corporations established research and development (R and D) components, which they promptly shut down at the end of the sixties when the government ended the tax incentives. The government's theory that the companies would get into the habit of innovating once they set up R and D units was disproven by experience. The dismal level of innovative activity in high-technology industries in Canada is revealed by the fact that between 1969 and 1971, of the 25,000 scientists and engineers graduated in Canada, only 2,000 got jobs in manufacturing. This represented a worsening trend; in the early sixties, half the graduates in these fields were hired by manufacturing firms.[14]

The ownership of Canadian resource and manufacturing industries by American corporations has provided the institutional basis for reducing Canada to a northern hinterland of the United States. During the fifties and early sixties, when American investment was widely regarded in Canada as the key to growth and prosperity, Canada's manufacturing industries were being steadily reduced to warehouse and assembly operations. Dependent on imported technology, and imported parts and components, most branch plants were incapable of producing an end-product from start to finish.

As long as the branch plant economy delivered higher living standards and economic growth, there was no significant Canadian opposition to American domination of the economy. There were the uneasy rumblings of Diefenbaker nationalism in the late fifties. But Canadians were not yet aware of the long-run fate that befalls a nation whose economy and whose state structures are controlled from the outside.

It was in the mid-sixties that Canadians began to awaken to the effects of U.S. control of their economy and their state institutions. By this date, more profits and dividends were flowing south than were being replaced with new foreign investment from the U.S. By the end of the sixties, American corporations were financing 90 per cent of their investment in Canada through the reinvestment of profits made in

Canada and through money borrowed on the Canadian money market.[15]

Also by the mid-sixties, the United States was running into serious difficulty in maintaining its domination of the world capitalist economy. Western European and Japanese industries were invading the American market and were providing stiff competition for American industries located outside the United States as well. While in 1960 the U.S. enjoyed a five billion dollar surplus in its manufacturing trade, in 1972 this had become a seven billion dollar deficit. And in the later years of the sixties, America's competitors achieved gigantic surpluses in their manufacturing trade: for example, West Germany, $16.4 billion and Japan, $19 billion.[16] The U.S. dollar's position as the reserve currency of the western world was at stake. In an earlier chapter we saw the significance of this deterioration of America's economic strength vis à vis Western Europe and Japan in necessitating a new energy strategy for America.

In Canada, the effect of America's new international position began to be felt by the late 1960s. First, American corporations, and later, the American state, took steps which changed the nature of the American presence in Canada. In 1966 American corporations began shifting their investments in manufacturing from Canada to western Europe. Their investments in Canadian resources were increased. The new international economic climate had made investments in manufacturing in Canada less attractive than other available alternatives.

A study of U.S. multi-national corporations produced for the U.S. Senate in February 1973, detailed the behaviour of U.S. firms abroad. The study examined the trends in employment in manufacturing in U.S.-owned multi-national corporations in seven countries: Canada, the United Kingdom, Belgium-Luxembourg, France, West Germany, Mexico and Brazil. Between 1966 and 1970, U.S. multi-nationals increased their share of manufacturing employment in these seven countries by an average of 25 per cent. The only country in which there was a decrease in the proportion of manufacturing workers employed by U.S. multi-nationals was Canada, and this decrease was not an indication of lessening U.S. control of the country's economy. It occurred at the same time as U.S. multi-nationals increased their share of sales in manufactured goods in the Canadian market.

Evaluating the evidence, the Senate study concluded that the drop in relative employment by U.S. multi-nationals in manufacturing in Canada "reflects the [multi-national corporations'] shift of the focus of their dynamic expansion away from Canada and toward other areas, chiefly western Europe."[17]

In the opinion of the study, U.S. multi-nationals had a marked negative impact on Canadian manufacturing employment between 1966 and 1970, the reverse of the pattern in every other case.[18]

A study of manufacturing employment in Ontario conducted by the Ontario Waffle produced similar results. The Waffle study demonstrated the difference in employment trends in large American-owned and large Canadian-owned firms in Ontario between 1966 and 1972. The study involved a sample of manufacturing establishments in Ontario employing one hundred or more workers. In the sample studied there was a marked difference in the behaviour of U.S.-owned and Canadian-owned firms.

Out of 511 U.S.-owned plants in the sample studied for both 1966 and 1972, 85 establishments shut down between 1966 and 1972 and 122 new ones opened up. Overall employment by the U.S. firms grew from 221,137 to 238,961 in this period, an increase of 8.1 per cent. The average size of establishment in this category of the sample increased from 371 employees to 377 employees.

There were 296 Canadian-owned plants studied for both 1966 and 1972. Thirty-five of them shut down between 1966 and 1972 and 75 new ones opened up. Overall employment in this sample of Canadian-owned firms grew from 106,900 to 129,513, an increase of 21.1 per cent. The average size of establishment in the sample increased from 323 employees to 349 employees.[19]

It is evident that while large firms increased their employment whether they were Canadian- or American-owned, there was almost three times as much employment growth in the Canadian-owned firms. American firms apparently passed on most of the new jobs created by their increased activity in Canada to the parents' plants in the U.S. or other foreign countries. This explains the enormous difference in the behaviour of the American- and Canadian-owned firms in the sample. The difference is clearly not explained by a U.S. withdrawal from the Ontario economy, as the significantly higher figure for U.S. plant openings over shutdowns attests.

The U.S. firms, as the U.S. Senate study showed, while increasing their dominance of the market, were cutting back their relative share of employment. This can best be explained by the growing tendency of U.S. firms to import parts and components manufactured by their U.S. operations into Canada for final assembly and retailing.

That U.S. manufacturing firms displace jobs abroad in the long run is acknowledged in the U.S. Senate study. The study concluded that a key role of U.S. multi-national corporations is to foster the sales of parts and components manufactured in the U.S. to branch plants abroad. The study estimated that this role far outweighs the importance of imports to the U.S. from the foreign operations of U.S. multi-nationals. The net employment gain to the U.S. from these operations of U.S. multi-nationals was placed at half a million.[20]

Although the study did not break down this figure of half a million jobs in terms of the foreign countries negatively affected, we can conclude that Canada tops the list. This is clear because Canada is the site of about 30 per cent of all direct U.S. investments abroad.[21] It is further evident in light of the U.S. Senate study's conclusion that Canada was the only country in which relative employment in U.S. multi-nationals engaged in manufacturing has been dropping.

An example of how the foreign operations of a U.S. firm actually reduced the number of jobs in the host country was reported in *Fortune* magazine:

> When Kimberly-Clark built a $23 million paper mill in Huntsville, Ontario to serve the Canadian market, it purchased enough equipment in the U.S. to supply 51 man-years of employment. Had Kimberly-Clark not built the mill, a Canadian competitor would have captured the market and bought less equipment in the U.S. (resulting in only 16 man-years of employment). As for the balance of payments, the investment resulted in no net outflow of capital, and as soon as Kimberly-Clark pays off a Canadian bank loan, the subsidiary expects to pay $2.8 million a year in dividends to the parent company in the U.S.[22]

Since the mid-1960s, the actions of U.S. multi-national corporations in Canada have further undermined the already weak manufacturing base of the country. The motive for U.S. manufacturing firms shifting new jobs to the U.S. was not patriotic concern for the employment of American workers—but production costs and profits. The U.S. Senate study on multi-national corporations concluded that the major reason U.S. corporations set up branch plants abroad is not to avail themselves of cheaper labour, but to capture the markets. In the Canadian case, the national market for many manufactured goods is divided among so many foreign firms that production costs tend to be relatively high. Once a position in the Canadian market has been secured, a U.S. firm has a clear interest in importing parts and components from the U.S. parent firm, whose production runs for the U.S. market are longer and costs per unit cheaper.

But while the individual U.S. firm is not concerned with the overall well-being of the American economy, the U.S. state is concerned precisely with this. The deteriorating trade position of the United States and the weakening of the U.S. dollar led the Nixon administration to undertake its new economic policies on August 15, 1971.

We have already examined the broad international implications of the Nixon programme in a previous chapter. Here we are concerned with the implications of Nixon's policies for Canada.

While U.S. government spokesmen often forget in public to acknowledge Canada's existence as a foreign, sovereign nation, this does not mean that the U.S. state overlooks Canada's role in American economic policies. When President Nixon remarked at a 1971 press conference that "Japan is our biggest customer in the world,"[23] he had not really forgotten that Canadian purchases from the U.S. come close to the value of the purchases of America's next four best customers—Japan, West Germany, Britain and France—combined.

While Canada is not the major cause of America's trade problems, it is clear that this country can be a major part of the solution. Since the launching of Nixonomics, the U.S. has had two overriding objectives in its dealings with Canada: to secure U.S. access to Canadian resources—especially energy resources—and increase Canadian imports of American manufactured goods.

As we have seen, Canadian dependence on imported machinery is a major factor ensuring that this country will continue to develop its resources in line with continental rather than Canadian demand. But from an economic or a political standpoint, there is one single pressure point that can be used as a precision instrument to guarantee Canadian compliance with American resource demands: the Canada-U.S. auto pact. We have already noted Donald Macdonald's remark in the fall of 1973, that Canada cannot eliminate its exports of oil to the United States without facing retaliation, perhaps in the form of cancellation of the auto pact.

The auto pact is the most important insurance the Americans have to protect them from any attempt to disrupt their ownership of the Canadian petroleum industry, or any move to prevent the development of Canadian oil and gas in line with continental demand.

Auto production is *the* central industry in Ontario, the nation's most industrialized province. At stake are not merely the 85,000 jobs in Canada's auto industry, but jobs in all the industries which supply the auto industry—steel, glass, plastics, textiles, electrical products and rubber.

The auto pact was the golden achievement of the federal Liberal government in the 1960s. It was the Pearson government's response to growing deficits in Canada's trade with the U.S., particularly in auto parts. (In 1965, the U.S. enjoyed a $768 million surplus in its auto trade with Canada.) The deteriorating condition of Canada's auto industry in the early sixties left the government with two basic choices: it could push for a single integrated auto industry on the North American continent or encourage the development of an all-Canadian auto industry, modelled on the western European experience.

The Liberal government chose the continental option. And, as we know from the U.S. Senate study on the multi-national corporation, the U.S. entered into the auto pact to *prevent* the evolution of a Canadian auto industry.

In 1965, the auto pact was undertaken as a means of rationalizing the North American automobile industry. Its goal was ultimate free trade in assembled autos and in auto parts. One continental auto market, serviced by giant American producers, was the vision. It meant that Canadian auto plants would not be geared to producing for the Canadian market. Instead they would produce for segments of the entire North American market.

To make this plunge into a continental economy more palatable to Canadians, the auto pact included a series of safeguards that guaranteed Canadians a proportion of North American auto production. The safeguards ensured that Canadian production would not fall below the 1964 level and would rise at least to the extent of 60 per cent of the increase in Canadian purchases of North American cars and 50 per cent of the increase in Canadian purchases of North American commercial vehicles. In addition, the auto companies agreed to pour extra investment, amounting to $250 million more than the safeguards in the pact guaranteed, into Canada between 1965 and 1968.

Under the auto pact the Canadian industry was rationalized to produce fewer lines of cars for the entire North American market. By 1968, imports of autos from the U.S. supplied more than 40 per cent of the Canadian market compared with 3 per cent in 1964; about 60 per cent of vehicles produced in Canada in 1968 were exported compared with 7 per cent in 1964. The auto pact soon accounted for one-third of all trade between Canada and the U.S.[24]

The early years of the auto pact seemed a shining success story for the concept of a continental economy. With rationalization of the industry in Canada, there was a marked increase in productivity in the Canadian industry and a transfer of management functions from Canada to the United States. Canada increased its share of North American auto production. In 1970 and 1971, for the first time, Canada had a small surplus in its auto trade with the U.S. (although even in these two years there was a Canadian deficit, counting the profits U.S. subsidiaries in this country sent home).

Growth in Canada's relative output in the industry was not matched by growth in Canadian auto jobs relative to the North American total. The proportion of Canadians to Americans employed remained exactly the same as it had been in 1964.

What was not immediately clear in the early years of Canadian success in the auto pact was that Canada had virtually given up the right to have any say in the future rate of growth in its own auto industry. Once Canada's auto industry was securely integrated into the continental framework, American pressures for revision of the pact began. These pressures came in the form of statements delivered in the U.S. Congress and President Nixon's call for removal of the Canadian safeguards from the auto pact.

But it was Nixonomics that really began the process of undermining Canada's auto industry. The DISC tax programme invited American corporations exporting goods from the U.S. to write off 50 per cent of the taxes on their foreign sales. This was an enormous inducement to the auto companies to export more to Canada from their American operations. While the list of companies making use of DISC is not public, the Ford Motor Company has acknowledged that it is taking advantage of the programme.

In 1972, Canada returned to a deficit position in its auto trade with the U.S. The deficit grew steeply to three hundred million dollars for the first three-quarters of 1973. Having digested the Canadian auto industry, the United States was now using it to help overcome American trade problems.[25]

The auto pact is the ideal pressure point for maintaining U.S. control of the Canadian economy. This is so because the importance of the pact is so much greater for Canada than for the U.S. Its cancellation would deny Canada access to 60 per cent of its present auto market and would cut off the flow of parts—without which this country could not produce *any* automobiles—to Canada.

It is not surprising that domestic American politicians who have not been housebroken as diplomats often publicly demand that the U.S. use the threat of cancelling the auto pact to bring Canada to terms on other issues, such as oil.

The guarantee of Canada's economic dependency tomorrow is to be found in the structure of the continental economy today. The American presence in Canada constantly recreates the conditions for future Canadian dependence.

In the winter months of 1974 the pattern of the future was made clear. Figures were released revealing that in December 1973 while the value of Canadian oil exports was up 52 per cent over the previous December, motor vehicle exports had dropped 25 per cent. As Canadian resource exports mounted in value, the proportion of North American auto industry capital investment going into Canada was falling sharply. In 1970, 13 per cent of new North American auto investment was located in Canada; by 1973 this had fallen to a dismal 5 per cent.[26] In February 1974, the *Financial Times* concluded:

If demand remains strong for Canada's primary exports, there will be a temptation to drop the search for an 'industrial strategy'—which was to give Canada an expanded and competitive manufacturing sector—and concentrate instead on a 'resource strategy' which would extract the maximum benefit from world shortages.[27]

The pattern is as follows: the Americans import increasing amounts of Canadian resources, thus creating a trade balance in Canada's favour; to offset this, the U.S. government takes steps to augment the already existing tendency of U.S. firms to export parts and components to their Canadian branch plants; in order to deal with the resultant sluggish growth in the manufacturing sector of the economy, Canadian governments turn to giant resource exporting projects such as the Mackenzie Valley pipeline and the James Bay hydro development. Dependence begets dependence. The reliance on resource-exporting projects involves giving away Canada's comparative advantage in cheaper materials, resulting in lower American industrial costs and higher Canadian industrial costs. This, in turn, heightens the tendency of American manufacturers to export parts produced in their American operations to their Canadian branch plants; and again, Canadian politicians fearful of the country's high unemployment rates look around for more of Canada to sell.

Now that the United States faces serious competition from Japan and western Europe, its need to rationalize Canada's position within its empire has been greatly increased. There is less margin to work with than there was in the good old days of "special status" for Canada within the American empire. Today, it is in the overriding interest of American capitalism that Canada increase its twin role as supplier of resources and consumer of manufactured goods.

American control of Canada's petroleum and auto industries is the linchpin in the continental economic structure. Their control by U.S. corporations and their integration into the continental economic system guarantee that Canadian governments will accept a high degree of de-industrialization.

Notes

[1]Report of the Materials Policy Commission (the Paley Report), *Resources for Freedom, the Outlook for Energy Sources* (Washington, D.C., U.S. Government Printing Office, 1952), v. 3, p. 6.

[2]Statistics Canada, *Canada Year Book, 1972* (Ottawa, 1972) pp. 1094-1095.

[3]*Ibid.*, p. 589.

[4]*Ibid.*, pp. 1086, 1090.

[5]Pierre L. Bourgault, *Innovation and the Structure of Canadian Industry,* background study for the Science Council of Canada, October 1972, Special Study No. 23, (Ottawa, 1972) p. 83.

[6]*Ibid.*, p. 51.

[7]This figure was arrived at by comparing statistics in the *Canadian Statistical Review* (published by Statistics Canada), for 1965 and 1971.

[8]U.S. Department of Commerce, Bureau of the Census, *Statistical Abstract of the United States 1972* (Washington, D.C., U.S. Department of Commerce, 1972) p. 219.

[9]Statistics from *Canada Year Book, 1972, op. cit.*, p. 776 and *Statistical Abstract of the United States, op. cit.*, p. 697.

[10]Statistics Canada, *Employment, Earnings, and Hours, August 1972* (Ottawa, 1972) p. 12.

[11]James Laxer, "Canadian Manufacturing and U.S. Trade Policy", in Robert Laxer, ed., *(Canada) Ltd.* (Toronto, McClelland and Stewart, 1973) p. 129.

[12]*Canada Year Book, 1972, op. cit.* p. 1090.

[13]Bourgault, *op. cit.*, p. 105.

[14]Science Council of Canada, *Innovation in a Cold Climate,* October 1971, Report No. 15, (Ottawa, 1971) p. 19.

[15]James Laxer, "Introduction to the Political Economy of Canada", in Robert Laxer, *op. cit.*, p. 36.

[16]Committee on Finance, United States Senate, report of, *Implications of Multinational Firms for World Trade and Investment and for U.S. Trade and Labor,* (Washington, D.C., U.S. Government Printing Office, 1973) p. 418.

[17]*Ibid.*, p. 615.

[18]*Ibid.*, p. 616.

[19]Jim Laxer and Doris Jantzi, "The De-industrialization of Ontario", in Robert Laxer, *op. cit.*, pp. 147-152.

[20]U.S. Senate Committee on Finance Report, *op. cit.*, p. 401.

[21]*Ibid.*, p. 406.

[22]*Fortune,* April 1972.

[23]Peter C. Newman, *Home Country* (Toronto, McClelland and Stewart, 1973) p. 229.

[24]*Canada Year Book, 1972, op. cit.*, p. 1065.

[25]*Globe and Mail,* March 19, 1974.

[26]*Financial Times,* February 18, 1974.

[27]*Ibid.*

12   A New Energy and Industrial Strategy for Canada

A powerful new nationalist mood is everywhere evident among Canadians. In the space of a few years Canadians have rejected the view that this country benefits from its ties with the United States. A substantial majority of Canadians want changes in the country's economic structure.

But the desire for national independence is not evenly distributed in the population. The issue of nationalism versus continentalism has polarized Canadians along class lines. The majority of Canadians who work for a salary or a wage want national independence; the minority, the nation's businessmen, are locked into support for continental economic integration.

Nationalist sentiment has arisen among the Canadian people as a result of the country's ill-balanced economic structure. Canada's role as resource base for the United States has prevented the full development of manufacturing in Canada. And limited industrial development has led to the country's inability to create new jobs at a rate sufficient to keep pace with the growth of the work force.

Furthermore, the retarded growth of the nation's manufacturing sector has resulted in the overdevelopment of the nation's service industries. Service industries include all categories of workers who do not produce commodities. Their role in the economy is to increase the efficiency of commodity production, or to merchandise the commodities that are produced. (For example, teachers and researchers train the labour force and prepare new techniques so that more efficient production can occur; advertisers, bankers, and retailers merchandise the commodities produced and organize the financing of future production.) In spite of the seemingly endless growth of service industry jobs, which now employ two-thirds of Canada's labour force, these jobs depend on the state of the nation's commodity-producing industries. With only one-third of the country's work force involved in producing commodities (food, mineral extraction, and manufacturing), there is a distinct limit to the number of service jobs the nation can support.

Canada's service industries are now seriously over-extended. Much of the service industry growth has been created through expanding the number of jobs under government auspices. Canadian governments have been world leaders in the art of playing the role of the nation's employer of last resort. It is entirely appropriate that Canada should be the home of makework projects such as the Local Initiatives Program (LIP) or Opportunities for Youth (OFY).

Today, Canadians pay the cost of having the most over-extended service sector of any economy in the western world. The costs include: an intolerably high rate of inflation, which results in part from government expenditure of more and more of the country's income to provide additional non-productive jobs; and falling real incomes for workers in the service industries because of the incapacity of the commodity-producing industries to support such a large service sector at high rates of pay.

All three levels of government now feel the pinch of the economy's bulging service sector. Recent government decisions to place ceilings on spending in education and health care are attempts to adjust to the structural imbalance of the economy. The rising militancy of teachers and hospital workers is a response to the same phenomenon.

Canada's branch plant economy is now providing few new manufacturing jobs; and the expansion of the service sector has been stretched to its limits. As a result, both manufacturing workers and workers in the service industries are now threatened with job insecurity and falling real incomes.

This new insecurity, which affects not only marginal, but central sections of the country's work force, is the outcome of Canada's role as resource supplier for the United States. It means that sections of the population who were, for the most part, the mass base of the nation's quiescent politics, are now becoming deeply disturbed about the direction of the economy.

Despite the discontent of Canadians, the demand for nationalist economic policies has not resulted in any basic alteration of the platform of any of the nation's major political parties. The late sixties and the early seventies has been a period of increasing nationalist rhetoric in Canadian politics. But the substance of political victory has gone to the continentalists. In the nation's three major political parties the results have been the same: the nationalists have been reduced to a position of weakness.

Conservative intellectuals like Donald Creighton and George Grant have made a crucial contribution to developing an analysis of Canada's dependent position in the American empire. But the Conservative Party does not reflect the views of either Creighton or Grant. The weight of the Alberta wing of the party, including the Lougheed government and a solid phalanx of MPs, ensures that the federal Tory party will remain the most uncompromising representative of the foreign-owned oil companies in national politics.

In the Liberal Party, the classical voice of continentalism in Canada, the nationalists have moved from failure to failure since the party's election to office in 1963. The long list of defeats for Walter Gordon in the Pearson cabinet and the absence of both Gordon and Eric Kierans from the present cabinet has placed undisputed power in the hands of the party's unalloyed pro-Americans, Mitchell Sharp and John Turner. Even if Energy Minister Donald Macdonald harbours any lingering vestiges of Walter Gordonism, Sharp and Turner can be expected to carry the cabinet with them on crucial matters.

In the NDP, ostensibly the most nationalist of the three parties, the expulsion of the party's Waffle group in Ontario and the Waffle's decision to leave the NDP in Saskatchewan left the federal party in the hands of the top officers of the American unions in Canada.

The Lewis leadership, both father and son, has virtually abandoned the independence issue. Stephen Lewis began the Ontario party's retreat on the energy issue from the moment he was elected leader in October 1970. Lewis ignored a Waffle-initiated resolution, adopted by the party's convention, which called on the NDP to campaign in opposition to a continental energy deal. Over the next two years Lewis successfully convinced the party to reverse another part of the same resolution, which had declared support for public ownership of the nation's energy resource industries. At the federal level, David Lewis, as noted in an earlier chapter, continued to back the Liberals even following Trudeau's declaration in favour of the Mackenzie Valley pipeline.

In addition, the NDP's remaining left wing has been uncertain on the independence issue. Its spokesman, B.C. Premier Dave Barrett, is responsible for one of the most continentalist gestures made by any Canadian premier on the energy issue. In early 1973, he held a press conference in Washington, D.C., to propose that the Americans ship their Alaskan oil across British Columbia to the lower forty-eight states. In effect, Barrett offered to turn his province into a land bridge between two parts of the United States.

The defeat of the nationalists within these political parties has been no accident. It happened in the Conservative and Liberal parties because both American and Canadian business in Canada are committed to a continental economic system. It happened in the NDP because the leaders of the American unions in Canada fear that the independence issue will lead to an irresistible sentiment in favour of Canadian unions.

The continentalism of the major parties contrasts with the growing desire of the Canadian people for national independence.

A Gallup poll taken in the spring of 1973 revealed the widening gap between the wishes of the Canadian public and their political representatives on the central issue of the nation's energy resources. The poll reported that 48 per cent of Canadians favour public ownership of energy resource industries as an alternative to leaving them in the hands of private, foreign owners. Only 36 per cent were reported as opposed to public ownership.[1] And this was the case despite the fact that public ownership of energy industries was not part of the platform of any of the major parties.

Though a new energy strategy is unlikely to emerge from within the major political parties, the results of the Gallup poll provide evidence that there is wide popular support for such a strategy.

A new energy strategy must come. If the nation's major parties fail to give voice to it, then new political institutions will arise to fill the vacuum that exists in Canadian politics.

A new energy strategy that responds to the needs of Canadians has to be based on a clear set of principles. As we saw in a previous chapter, the federal government's June 1973 energy report outlined five options for Canadian energy development during this decade, with price tags ranging from forty-two billion dollars for self-sufficiency to sixty-eight billion dollars for maximum development of export projects.

The evidence is overwhelming that the export of energy has a seriously distorting effect on the Canadian economy. The first principle in a new Canadian energy strategy must be the development of Canadian energy resources in response to Canadian needs and not for export.

The adoption of the self-sufficiency approach would ensure that Canadians are provided with energy at the lowest possible cost and would eliminate the need to import foreign capital for energy development. In the aftermath of the world oil price revolution of 1973, a self-sufficiency model based on the following policy elements is needed:

- The immediate construction of an all-Canadian oil pipeline from western Canada to Montreal, capable of carrying sufficient crude to eliminate imports of higher-priced overseas oil into eastern Canada.
- Exploration of east coast offshore fields to provide eastern

Canada with crude oil and natural gas from this region.
● The phasing out of all oil and natural gas exports to the United States.
● The gradual development of the Alberta oil sands for Canadian needs with no undertakings to export oil sands production.
● A moratorium on the building of a Mackenzie Valley natural gas pipeline and a refusal to undertake any additional natural gas exports.

But simply setting out the self-sufficiency approach is not adequate. Of crucial importance is the question of who is to preside over the implementation of a new energy strategy for Canada. The foreign-owned oil companies have acted as private governments, making decisions on the development of Canada's energy resources in response to continental rather than Canadian need. They have presided over the export of much of Canada's low cost oil and gas; their activities have enhanced American rather than Canadian industrial development; and they have produced handsome profits for their foreign owners that now exceed the amount of new foreign capital flowing into Canada for energy development.

The oil companies in Canada have teamed up to scare the public into accepting development schemes which are not needed by Canadians. Their consistent approach has been to avoid competition in order to fatten their profits. And when faced with proposals for price freezes or higher taxes, they have used the thinly veiled threat that they will restrict supply if any attempt is made to curtail their price-gouging practices.

With their long record of acting against the interests of the Canadian people, the oil companies can have no part of a new strategy for Canada. A crucial principle in a new strategy must be complete public ownership of the nation's energy resource industries. Only public ownership will ensure the pursuit of a strategy in the interest of the majority of Canadians.

If public ownership is needed, then how should it be achieved?

Two key factors should determine the level of compensation to be paid to the oil companies in bringing them under public ownership. First, the oil resources over which they preside are *already publicly owned*. Under the British North America Act, resources are a part of the public domain. They can be leased to private corporations, but their ownership can never be alienated. To pay compensation for the estimated worth of the resources would be absurd, since the resources already belong to the people.

What about compensation for the investments undertaken by the oil companies to develop the resource? As we saw in a previous chapter, the largest single source of investment capital for the oil companies comes from the tax write-offs they enjoy. For the past fifteen years the public, through forgone taxes, has been putting up twice as much development capital as have the foreign owners of the oil companies. And while the foreign owners have been taking a dividend out of Canada larger than the new provision of foreign capital, the public has not received a nickel for its huge investment.

The fact is that the Canadian people have already paid full compensation to the oil companies and their foreign owners do not deserve a penny more.

But while paying compensation to the foreign oil companies would amount to double compensation, that is not the case with the individual shareholders who have investments in the oil industry. These individual investors, who hold a small portion of the ownership of the oil companies, should be compensated immediately and in full when public ownership is implemented.

The goal of publicly owned energy industries pursuing a strategy of Canadian energy self-sufficiency makes sense only as an element in a new industrial strategy. Phasing out exports of energy resources would create the opportunity to develop manufacturing industries. Ending energy exports means reserving Canada's lowest cost energy sources for domestic use to provide a comparative advantage for Canadian industry. In addition, eliminating the outflow of dividends and profits to foreign owners would maximize the availability of development capital for Canadian industry. The adoption of the self-sufficiency model means that capital can be used for industrial development in Canada, not siphoned off into projects for resource exports.

A new industrial strategy should involve reducing Canada's imports of finished products to provide a new domestic market for the nation's manufacturing output. If Canada set as a goal for this decade the lowering of Canadian per capita imports of manufactured goods to the American per capita level of imports, a new annual market of more than eight billion dollars would be available to Canadian industry. Supplying this market would create enough new jobs in manufacturing and in related service industry development to eliminate unemployment in Canada.

Public ownership of Canada's oil industry can only be achieved if the country is determined to embark on a broad new industrial strategy at the same time. Canada's trained manpower, extensive and varied resources, and potential for manufacturing are such that the country is capable of achieving full economic independence from the United States. Only such a new strategy, geared to ending Canada's industrial dependence on the United States, would guarantee success in the face of likely American attempts to retaliate against Canada's nationalization of the oil industry.

Highest priority would go to the development of the nation's skilled manpower to provide a new source of technology. In addition large investments would be needed to create an independent machinery industry to provide Canada with the equipment needed for a full industrial economy. Furthermore, such a strategy would necessitate the willingness of Canada to create an all-Canadian auto industry geared to producing for the Canadian market.

Another key element in a new industrial strategy must be the decentralization of the location of manufacturing industries. At present 80 per cent of Canada's manufacturing is located in a narrow band of central Canada stretching from Windsor to Montreal. Ending Canada's role as resource hinterland can only occur if substantial industrialization is undertaken in the country's primary producing regions. Western Canada, northern Ontario, eastern Quebec and the Atlantic provinces must be the priority regions for the location of new manufacturing.

A key goal in a new industrial strategy must also be the elimination of wasteful production. In our present social system, goods are produced because they are profitable, not because they meet human needs. This leads to the squandering of material resources and human labour.

Why should we Canadians embark on such bold departures in our energy and industrial strategy?

We should because we must if we are to avoid being prisoners in an American economic machine, during a decade of gigantic struggle for power among the great industrial nations. The energy crisis is a product of that struggle. In the coming world economic upheaval, Canada will be defenceless as the northern frontier of an American empire that is itself in serious economic difficulty.

We should because a new energy and industrial strategy can mean that for the first time the people on the northern half of this continent can make their own history, and can become full, creative human beings, in a self-determining society.

We should, because to take such a step means embarking on a course that will lead to a new socialist society in Canada based on equality of the human condition, in which exploitation of people for private profit is eliminated.

Notes

[1] Toronto *Star*, April 18, 1973.

13　Energy Crisis Update: The Oil Companies' New Energy Policy for Canada

Until 1973, the foreign-owned petroleum industry in Canada pursued a consistent strategy that was well understood by Canadians. The industry's goal was rapid development of production through the extension of its markets, particularly in the United States. The Canadian branch of the American oil industry shipped petroleum to Ontario markets through a pipeline that delivered half of its supply to American markets along the way.

In 1973, the Canadian petroleum industry entered a new and mysterious phase in its development. The industry dropped its traditional rhetoric about expanding production and began predicting petroleum shortages for Canada. The whole of Canadian economic strategy was threatened by the gloomy new forecasts. And not the least mysterious aspect of the situation was the almost universally uncritical acceptance of the new picture being painted by the petroleum industry. This chapter is about the oil industry's new forecasts—why they have been made and what they mean for Canada.

In the space of a single year the oil companies drastically changed their estimates of Canada's potential for producing oil. In 1973, the oil companies told us that Canada could produce more than enough oil to meet her domestic needs for the next eighty years. In 1974, they told us that Canada would face domestic oil shortages in only eight years.

This dramatic change in estimates took place at the same time as the international price of oil increased from three dollars a barrel to eleven dollars a barrel. The coincidence of these two developments — the change in the estimates of Canada's reserves and the international oil price revolution — must give pause to any serious observer. Projected oil shortages in Canada are welcome news to the oil industry. They serve to prod governments to raise the domestic price of Canadian oil to the world price.

137

Despite the disturbing coincidence of these events, the Canadian government has gone along unquestioningly with the new estimates of the industry. It has done so, at least in part, because only the oil companies are equipped organizationally to make a thorough inventory of the nation's reserves. Government agencies and the public are prisoners of a small group of petroleum companies who have a monopoly on this information and whose top level decision-making is located outside Canada—in American and European offices.

The projected petroleum shortages imply the need for a revision in the nation's economic priorities. If the new estimates of the oil industry are correct, Canadians will be required to make enormously greater investments in energy developments than they expected to make only a few years ago. Moreover, assumptions about the nation's industrial potential may have to undergo significant alteration.

The problem is that the petroleum industry controls a vital building block on which our entire industrial structure is based. Its monopoly of the technology, the equipment, the organization and the information which makes possible the extraction of petroleum gives it unparalleled power to influence the nation's economic strategy.

The new projections of the petroleum industry are too obviously self-serving to be accepted at face value. These projections have been used to turn Canadian energy policy upside down. The petroleum industry has all but smashed the two-price system in Canada with its lower domestic oil prices; it has helped itself to record profits; and it is now making vast deals with governments for the development of the Alberta oil sands and Arctic oil and natural gas.

It is these projections which make Canada's energy situation in mid-1975 appear so different from what it seemed to be eighteen months earlier, when the earlier chapters of this book were written. In that intervening eighteen-month period, the oil companies have made giant strides toward implementing the international oil price revolution in Canada — in spite of the obvious national interest in the industrial advantage which lower oil prices give the Canadian economy, in spite of the fact that every Canadian consumer pays once, and often twice and three times over, for any oil price increase, and in spite of the large and growing profits which the foreign-owned oil companies are already making in Canada. This chapter will examine the oil companies' strategy during this key eighteen-month period and analyse government response at the federal and provincial levels to this power play.

Smashing the two-price system

On a world scale, the major petroleum companies and the governments of oil-producing countries have used their monopoly power to achieve a revolution in the price of oil. These partners in monopoly, the oil companies and the major oil-exporting countries, exercised the power they accumulated throughout the 1960s, to achieve the price revolution of 1973. By restricting the rate of development of new oil-producing facilities, they eliminated surplus oil capacity which had allowed consuming countries to hold down the price of oil for the preceding twenty years.

While the oil price revolution has been achieved through the efforts of the major oil companies in concert with the Organization of Petroleum Exporting Countries, the oil-producing countries have made the greater relative gains. OPEC countries have stepped up their take on a barrel of oil from about two dollars at the end of 1972 to about eight dollars in 1974. The major oil companies, while recording record profits, have only doubled their take as a result of the price revolution. The impressive new strength of OPEC threatens the oil companies with a reduction in their power. To escape this fate the major oil companies are making frantic efforts to increase their oil reserves outside countries belonging to OPEC. Oil deposits in the North Sea, the Pacific, off the U.S. east coast and in the Canadian Arctic take on an increased significance as non-OPEC reserves.

For the oil companies, enlarged production capacity in these non-OPEC areas increases the clout of the companies in dealing with OPEC members. This is the case because both the companies and OPEC members have an interest in preventing a surplus supply of oil from coming on the market and driving down the price. At the very least, building their non-OPEC reserves gives the oil companies an assured future in areas not dominated by governments intent on battling the companies for every cent of the take.

The oil price revolution has had an enormous impact on the economies of western countries. It has fed the fires of inflation, pushing up gasoline and home-heating prices and driving up the price of food and industrial products as a result of higher fuel and raw material costs for agriculture and for industry. The price revolution has been a major factor in causing the most severe international recession since the 1930s. Higher fuel prices have directly affected the markets for durable consumer goods such as automobiles and electrical appliances throughout the western world. The price revolution has threatened the major industrial powers with the prospect of perennial trade deficits as a result of their dependence on imported oil.

In addition, the price revolution has radically altered the profitability of producing oil in various parts of the world. At eleven dollars a barrel, it is possible to produce oil in areas where it would be unprofitable at three dollars a barrel. Oil industry investment capital quite naturally flows to areas where the potential return is greatest. Countries that attempt to hold out against the price revolution find the oil companies moving elsewhere or threatening to move elsewhere. In Canada, producer of only 3 per cent of the world's oil, the price revolution has completely altered the behaviour of the oil companies domestically.

The Canadian situation is a microcosm of the oil industry's worldwide strategy. The uniqueness of the Canadian case though, has required unique features in this strategy. Apart from the United States, Canada is the only major western industrial country that is also a major oil producer. As a nation capable of meeting most, if not all of its oil needs through indigenous supplies, Canadians cannot easily be told that they must pay the world price for their oil simply because that is what the OPEC countries have dictated. Canadians have been told that they have plentiful supplies of energy resources for too long for them to accept a single jump to the world price. And yet the major oil companies have a genuine problem in Canada. Since the world price of oil has shot up far past the domestic Canadian price, the relative profitability of oil ventures in Canada has declined markedly. For oil companies concerned with maximum profits, lower prices for oil in Canada quite literally shrink the size of Canadian reserves worth developing in relation to reserves elsewhere in the world, because the profits to be made elsewhere are suddenly so much larger.

From their point of view, the oil companies need the world oil price for their Canadian production to make major new exploration ventures in this country attractive. To convince Canadians of the need for the world price, the oil companies have turned their estimates of Canadian oil "producibility" (the oil industry's term for potential production) upside down.

To understand what the oil companies have done in Canada it is necessary to review the sudden transition from their optimistic estimates of early 1973 to their pessimistic estimates made only a few months later.

In early 1973, Canadians still lived in a world of petroleum plenty. That the industry maintained its optimistic estimate of Canadian petroleum producibility early in 1973 is evident from two events: first, the response of the oil industry to the federal government's establishment of oil export controls, and second, the publication of the government's comprehensive energy report.

In February 1973, the federal government asserted its jurisdiction over the movement of Canadian oil across interprovincial and international boundaries by establishing crude oil export controls to begin on March 1.[1] The government took the action because it feared that

American demand for Canadian petroleum could potentially increase so rapidly that the Canadian petroleum industry would be unable to meet it. That the government's establishment of export controls was initially merely an assertion of jurisdiction is evident from the fact that to begin with the quota on exports was set at virtually the maximum capacity of the Interprovincial Pipeline that carried oil from western Canada to American and Ontario markets.[2]

Significantly, the oil industry and the Alberta government responded to the federal government's action by declaring that Canada's oil surplus was so large that no export controls were required.

In June 1973, the industry's last important assertion of its traditional optimism was seen in the report of the Department of Energy, Mines and Resources, entitled *An Energy Policy for Canada* (discussed earlier in this book). Like previous and subsequent government reports, the assessment of the prospects of the petroleum industry was based mainly on the industry's own evaluation of the situation. As noted in Chapter 6 of this book, the report told Canadians that although conventional oil production in the western provinces would begin to decline in the late 1970s, new sources of supply in the Canadian Arctic and in the oil sands would be entirely sufficient to prevent any shortfall from occurring. It made two estimates of Canadian oil producibility, one more optimistic than the other. The optimistic estimate predicted that Canadian oil output could increase steadily to a peak of over ten million barrels a day by the year 2000. Of this amount, eight million barrels a day could be produced with oil prices of less than six dollars a barrel. The less optimistic estimate predicted that Canadian oil output could increase steadily to six million barrels a day by the year 2000, and at prices of less than six dollars a barrel.[3]

This report was relegated to the cobwebs of history within a few weeks of being published. Spectacular changes were beginning in the world petroleum situation. Rumours of potential oil supply interruption due to the deteriorating political situation in the Middle East and speculations concerning impending oil price increases were pushing the American government toward proclaiming the goal of energy self-sufficiency as an urgent national priority. Self-sufficiency to the Americans meant new North American energy supplies, including non-conventional Canadian reserves in the Alberta oil sands and in the Arctic. The talk of U.S. self-sufficiency pointed toward much higher oil prices as the basis for the more intensive exploitation of petroleum reserves in North America.

Faced with impending oil price increases, the Canadian government took a step that was to prove popular with the Canadian people, but extremely unpopular with the oil companies—it established a two-price system for Canadian oil in September 1973. The two-price system was to consist of a fixed domestic price and an export price that moved upward with the going international price. The domestic price that was initially established was four dollars a barrel. The export tax, or the differential between the frozen Canadian price and the going price of other oil imports into the Chicago market, was first set at forty cents a barrel.[4]

As the price of other oil imports into the Chicago market rose over the next few months, the export tax rose by equivalent amounts. It was raised to $1.90 a barrel in December 1973; to $2.20 a barrel in January 1974 and to $6.40 a barrel in February 1974.[5]

The establishment of the two-price system was a brilliant political stroke on the part of the minority Liberal government. It promised Canadians relief from steep increases in the price of fuel just at the time when a Statistics Canada publication revealed that in the summer of 1973 the real incomes of Canadians fell for the first time since World War II.

The two-price system was popular in Canada for another reason. Lower oil prices in Canada provided Canadian industry with a definite advantage compared with industry located in the United States. In high-energy-using industries like chemicals, steel and paper, this was especially true. In general, it was a factor of significance for all heavy manufacturing industries. Logically, the two-price system fitted into an industrial strategy for Canada based on the promotion of domestic manufacturing industries. The two-price system was advantageous for the Liberals in a time of political uncertainty when their hard-pressed minority government faced the possibility of defeat if the Conservatives and the NDP could get together in the House of Commons. The two-price system identified the Liberals with the problems of consumers. Both the Conservatives and the NDP, on the other hand, had the misfortune to be associated with provincial governments in the country's oil-producing provinces, the Conservatives in Alberta, the NDP in Saskatchewan. Unlike the Liberals, these parties were implicated in the oil-producing provinces' support for higher oil prices.

Not surprisingly, the oil industry was strongly hostile to the two-price system. From the moment the system was established, the overriding purpose of the petroleum industry was to destroy it and to force Canadian oil prices upward to the export price.

That the oil industry would fight to end the two-price system was evident from the beginning. But that the oil industry would go to the length of totally altering its estimates of the producibility of oil in Canada to achieve this end was a more breathtaking strategy than most observers—this author included—foresaw at the time (see the discussion in Chapter 9, pages 86-95).

The oil industry's response to the domestic freeze on the price of oil was immediate, and in the long run, exceedingly effective. Within days of the freeze, the oil industry geared up its vast propaganda apparatus to undertake a turn-around in its public posture on the prospects of Canada's petroleum industry. The Canadian Petroleum Association and the oil companies put aside their earlier rosy forecasts and deluged the financial press with reports of impending energy shortages for Canada.

The publicity apparatus of the oil industry and the nation's highly receptive financial press attacked the two-price system on two fronts: first, they contended that higher oil prices were needed as an incentive to the industry to ensure sufficient exploration to meet the country's future energy needs; and second, they scaled down previous estimates of how long existing reserves would meet the country's requirements. Both of these attacks led to the same conclusion: without the incentive of higher prices and an end to the two-price system, Canadians could themselves face oil shortages in the not-so-distant future.

In the spring of 1974, the campaign for higher prices achieved its first major success. The federal government, having consulted the governments of Alberta and Saskatchewan, increased the price of Canadian crude oil from $4.00 to $6.50 a barrel. The two-price system remained, but the differential between the domestic price and the international price was beginning to shrink. As a corollary of the declining difference between the domestic and the world price, the export tax on oil sold to the United States declined by an equivalent of $2.50 a barrel.[6]

The price rise came as good news both to the American oil industry and to the American government. For the oil industry it meant higher profits. For the American government it meant that the differential between Canadian and American oil prices was disappearing. The American government had complained loudly about the export tax on Canadian oil sales, not as most people thought, because they expected Canada to sell oil to the U.S. at less than the world price, but because they wanted equally high prices for Canadian oil in Canada. The two-price system in Canada presented the American government with the unattractive reality of an incentive to industry to locate north of the border. In a world whose problem was becoming that of surplus industrial capacity this was not an attractive development. The price rise in the spring of 1974 eased relations between Washington and Ottawa. It reassured the U.S. that the two-price system was the temporary phenomenon Liberal cabinet ministers said it was, and that it would disappear when the difficulties of minority government in Canada were out of the way.

The battles against the two-price system in the fall and winter of

1973-74 proved to be mere preliminary skirmishes. The decisive engagement came in a series of hearings held by the National Energy Board in April and May of 1974 in Calgary, Vancouver and Ottawa on the question of Canadian oil exports. Received by the government in October 1974 and released a month later, the NEB report on exports that followed the hearings dealt the decisive blow to the two-price system.[7]

The NEB report contained estimates from the oil industry and government agencies on the producibility of Canadian oil from traditional conventional sources as well as from the Alberta oil sands and the Arctic. The report gave official credence to the oil industry's claim that Canada faced petroleum shortages in the near future. It involved a drastic downward revision of the estimates of Canadian oil producibility from the previous energy report of June 1973. The previous report had concluded that ''there is little question that Canada can satisfy her own needs easily until the year 2050 at oil prices reaching $7 or $8.''[8] The new report recorded a remarkably altered consensus. The most optimistic estimate presented in the new report was far more pessimistic than the least optimistic one contained in the old report. A sudden, extraordinary change of view had occurred.

The NEB, for its part, came up with estimates that fitted into the general range of the industry estimates presented on Canadian producibility. The federal government agency was therefore doing little more than reflecting the new consensus of the industry. Instead of predicting that Canada could meet its needs easily until 2050, the NEB concluded that demand for Canadian crude oil would exceed supply in 1982.

The NEB reached this conclusion on the basis of the following forecast: conventional oil producibility would decline from 2040 thousand barrels a day in 1975 to 1290 thousand barrels a day in 1982, oil sands producibility would increase from 60 thousand barrels a day in 1975 to 220 thousand barrels a day in 1982. The NEB therefore concluded that between 1975 and 1982, Canadian oil producibility would decline from 2100 thousand barrels daily to 1510 thousand barrels daily.[9]

The NEB estimated that Canadian demand for indigenous crude oil and pentanes would increase from 1205 thousand barrels a day in 1975 to 1530 thousand barrels a day in 1982. Both these figures assumed that Canadian crude oil would supply the market west of the Ottawa valley and would supply 250 thousand barrels a day to Montreal refineries, after the extension to Montreal of the Interprovincial Pipeline. It was assumed that the balance of the market east of the Ottawa Valley would be supplied with overseas crude oil from Venezuela and the Middle East. By 1982, the NEB estimated, demand for crude oil east of the Ottawa Valley would amount to 1200 thousand barrels a day. Therefore, Canada would need to import 950 thousand barrels of crude oil daily to meet its eastern Canadian needs.[10]

By 1982, according to the NEB figures, Canadian producibility would lag behind the demand for indigenous crude. A shortfall would result, leaving Canada with no crude for export and with the need to supplement its supplies of crude with additional imports. By 1982, Canada would be a net importer of about a million barrels a day of crude oil.[11]

Where did the enormous differences between the 1973 and 1974 estimates come from? They resulted from a significant downward revision of the estimate of producibility of conventional crude oil in the Prairies as well as a downward revision of how much oil sands production the nation could expect by the early 1980s. But the biggest difference between the two estimates came from the remarkable fact that in 1974 the NEB assumed no production of oil from the Canadian Arctic. In the 1973 report, Arctic oil was a major part of the supply picture for the future, with estimated reserves far in excess of those in the prairie pools of conventional resources. The 1974 report, though, assumed that there would be no frontier oil available at all by the early 1980s. The report concluded:

Clearly, additional exploratory and evaluation drilling is required before established reserves and producibility can be assigned to frontier areas. The Board considers it unlikely that oil from these areas will be available in substantial volume within the next ten years. The Board further considers this ten-year period to be crucial in any current appraisal of the need to protect Canadian oil supply. Accordingly no further consideration was given to future producibility of frontier reserves for the purposes of this report.[12]

On the basis of its estimate of Canadian producibility, the NEB report canvassed three potential options with respect to Canada's oil exports to the United States: Canada could continue its exports with no restrictions; immediately halt all further exports; or it could arrive at a formula for lessening exports. The report outlined at some length its rationale for choosing the option of lessening exports. (Readers who are interested in the criteria involved in establishing the formula used to determine exports, including the use of the formula for 1975, should turn to Appendix I.)

The NEB report concluded with the presentation of its estimate of how the export figure would decline step by step to a mere five thousand barrels a day in 1982, the year when Canadian demand for indigenous crude would exceed potential producibility.[13]

The publication of the report created a political sensation in Canada. Since 1961, the growth of the export market for Canadian crude had been the central feature of Canadian energy policy. Now it appeared that this feature of continental energy policy was about to come to an end. In implementing the recommendations in the NEB report, the government fixed January 1, 1975 as the date when exports of crude oil to the U.S. would begin to be phased out. Rather than setting the export figure for the first months of 1975 at 653 thousand barrels a day, however, (the figure arrived at through the NEB formula), the government fixed the export ceiling at 800 thousand barrels a day, a figure that marked a reduction of only 100 thousand barrels a day from the export level in the fall of 1974.[14]

Taken at face value, the NEB report of October 1974 appeared to be a responsible statement of public policy, drawing conclusions for Canadian policy based on the facts as the NEB understood them. The NEB had been presented with new evidence that made it appear that the nation faced a crisis of domestic oil producibility that would force Canada to step up oil imports in the near future. Presented with this prospect, the NEB had announced that Canada's oil exports would have to be phased out between 1975 and 1982.

But it is difficult to take the NEB report at face value. The NEB report asks us to believe that between June 1973 and October 1974 the consensus of opinion in the oil industry and in government agencies changed from an optimistic estimate of Canadian oil producibility to an extremely pessimistic one. This requires us to believe that a veritable revolution of geological scholarship occurred during this short period of time, erasing all memories of the techniques previously used to estimate the nation's oil producibility. Furthermore, it appears that the "new geology" was so convincing that all of the oil companies and government agencies that presented evidence to the NEB hearings had been converted to the new view at the same time. This, of course, is possible. But the previous experience of Canada and other countries with the major oil companies should lead us to look for other, more likely explanations of this change.

To do so, consider the situation Canada was in at the end of 1973 from the point of view of the oil companies. Clearly Canada was unlikely to be a tough, long-lasting holdout against the oil price revolution. Producing only 3 per cent of the world's oil, and with its oil supplies firmly under the control of American and western European majors, Canada was not in a position to mount a strong resistance. What was required for the oil companies to win their case was the construction of a publicly credible argument which would make an increase in Canadian oil prices seem reasonable, even necessary. To do this directly—to suggest that oil company profits were now so high in other countries of the world where the new international price prevailed that Canada would likewise have to increase its price levels to keep the oil companies here and keep them interested in finding and producing more oil—might have roused public sentiment against the oil companies. It might have led to demands that the oil companies be taken over by government, and be made to heed Canadian interests first.

Increased profits could, however, be obtained indirectly by a route much less likely to provoke public resistance: by introducing the intermediate step of a possible oil shortage in Canada. If it appeared that Canada's oil reserves were running out, then the public would probably be more willing to accept higher prices. This would be true especially if immediately following the implementation of these higher prices, the oil companies were to announce that Canada again had more than enough oil, and that the higher prices had stimulated the discovery of important new producible reserves.

Against that sketched-out scenario, it is interesting to compare the events of late 1974 and 1975. The first major move was the publication in October 1974 of the new NEB forecasts, which suggested the possibility of an oil shortage by the early-1980s.

The NEB report had formal responsibility for making recommendations with regard to exports, not with regard to prices. While the report pointed to the obvious conclusion that an oil price increase was needed, it did not state that conclusion. However, another report issued in the fall of 1974 did just that—the eleventh annual report of the Economic Council of Canada.

Although not formally a government body, the Council is an influential institution that was established by the government. The Council report recommended that Canada move to eliminate the two-price system for domestic oil production; Canada should allow domestic oil prices to rise to the world level. And in a not unrelated recommendation, the Economic Council maintained that between 1974 and the early 1980s Canada should seek to double the rate of inflow of new foreign investment into the country. This, the Council stated, would allow the country to maintain a satisfactory rate of economic growth, based on intensive resource industry development.[15]

By the end of 1974, most observers had concluded that the two-price system was dead—that it would be eliminated in two price rises, one in the spring of 1975 to $8.50 a barrel and a further rise the following spring to the world price of about eleven dollars.

Events in the early months of 1975 supported this speculation. In February, Prime Minister Trudeau met with Alberta Premier Peter Lougheed in Calgary to discuss the price of oil. They agreed that the price of Canadian crude was about to go up, but to what level they would not speculate. [16] Within days of the meeting the federal government removed voluntary restraints that had been established on the price of petroleum products in the fall of 1973. Imperial Oil immediately responded with an increase of 2.2 cents a gallon in the wholesale price of gasoline and heating oil. [17]

Beyond the two-price system — New exports

The oil industry predicted shortages in Canada in order to drive up the domestic price of Canadian petroleum. A corollary of the new estimates of the industry was this: If the nation faced potential shortages, clearly there was no room for large-scale petroleum exports to the United States. The NEB report acted on this corollary in October 1974, when it announced that oil exports would be phased out in stages between 1975 and 1982.

Do the new estimates mean the end of exports? Only if one assumes that the oil industry will not produce a *newer* set of estimates once the world price has been reached in Canada.

In all its predictions of potential shortages for Canada the oil industry has always left open one critical rider: given sufficient *economic* incentives the industry could be expected to improve its level of performance enormously. Canadian government reports on energy always make this assumption as well. The 1973 energy report was careful to demonstrate that successive price rises would continually enlarge the oil reserves that could be effectively tapped in the oil sands and in the frontier areas. [18] In other words, reserve figures and producibility estimates are not calculations of physical quantities, they are *economic assessments* of what can be produced at any given time. And since the attractiveness of producing at any given price in Canada is related to the level of returns the oil industry can realize globally, it follows that the higher the world price goes, the less attractive Canadian production will be at any price frozen below that level. In the planning of the oil industry, Canadian oil reserves can readily shrink or expand, depending on the relation of the domestic price to the world price. The NEB recognized this in its report of October 1974 when it made it clear that it regarded *economic factors* rather than *technological problems* as the key to Canadian producibility. In the midst of its gloomy forecasts, the October 1974 report recorded the NEB's ultimate faith in Canada's vast energy resources, provided the price is right. The report stated:

> Various studies of geologically potential oil, gas and other resources leave little doubt that there are abundant deposits in widely scattered

areas of Canada. The conversion of known resources, such as the oil sands and heavy oils, and inferred or potential resources, such as are expected in the frontier areas, into established reserves will require technological progress, but, more importantly, will require favourable economic conditions for development, production and transportation. . . . given sufficient lead-time and proper economic incentives, there is a good prospect that Canada could become self-sufficient in energy for a long period.[19]

To a large extent we are dealing with self-fulfilling prophecies. Once the Canadian price has been raised to the world level, the oil companies can claim that the incentive has paid off and that vast new oil reserves have been discovered. In fact, they can claim that the new discoveries have been so large that a new surplus has been created. The argument will then be that joint Canadian-American energy projects involving new Canadian exports are justified, because this way the Americans can help pay for the transportation systems to move the oil to market, thus lowering the per unit cost of fuel.

While we cannot expect this scenario to develop fully before the Canadian price of oil reaches the world level, there are *already* signs that its development is on the agenda. Federal Minister of Energy Donald Macdonald and observers in the business community have made forecasts that point to a new export strategy once the domestic price revolution is complete. In a newsletter to investors in January 1975, Richardson Securities of Canada made precisely this connection between world-level oil prices for Canada and exports to the U.S. Richardson Securities made the following forecast:

The obvious next step in the design of an energy policy and the solution of the taxation disputes is an agreement to raise the domestic price of crude oil to the prevailing international price level. . . . With Canada's existing oil reserves rapidly depleting, it makes no sense to hold domestic prices at a level that encourages consumption and discourages exploration and development of new reserves. . . . Now there is no reason to continue sheltering Canadian consumers from the higher world price level, either politically or economically, since most Canadians can plainly see the choice between low prices and declining supplies or higher prices and rising supplies of oil. There is not much doubt about which they would choose. As a result, when the pricing agreement comes up for renewal in the spring it is virtually certain that the domestic price will be moved up closer to the international level, probably by $2.00 – $2.50 per barrel. This will undoubtedly be followed by a further increase to the international level over the next year. . . . This should then mean a substantial upswing in exploration and development expenditures in the 1976-1978 period. Also, it would allow the removal of the export tax and serve to improve relations with the United States by raising at least a slim prospect of continued oil exports if sufficient reserves can be found and developed by the 1980's.[20]

On February 7, 1975, Federal Energy Minister Donald Macdonald revealed how temporary the pessimistic estimates of Canadian oil producibility could be. In reply to a question in the House of Commons, he stated that he anticipated that Canada would have an oil surplus again by 1985.[21] In October 1974, the NEB had projected the beginning of a deficit for Canada in 1982. But, the NEB had projected the deficit to continue for the whole of the forecast period, right down to 1993. Now, four months later, the projected shortfall had shrunk from an indefinite period beginning in 1982 to a period of only three years. Accounting for his new found optimism, Macdonald said: ''There is an active exploration programme under way both off-shore and in the Canadian Arctic and, indeed, this winter we have been encouraged by some substantial finds within the federal territories.''[22]

Given all the solemnity that surrounded the NEB's announced phaseout of exports to the U.S. between 1975 and 1982, Canadians are not sufficiently aware of how easily the NEB's export formula will respond to more optimistic future producibility forecasts from the industry.

To demonstrate this is not difficult. Keeping in mind that all of the industry estimates presented in the NEB report were down sharply from earlier estimates, the most conservative analysis would conclude that the stimulus of higher prices will bring estimates back to the point of at least the most optimistic levels contained in the NEB report. Using the most optimistic estimates presented to the NEB for Canadian oil producibility, the shortfall projected for 1982 would not occur in that year or in any subsequent year before 1990. If financial analysts who are predicting that Canadian crude will reach the world price in 1976 are correct, we could expect upward revisions in producibility estimates in time for setting the export level for 1977. Using the industry's most optimistic estimates for the next decade, the NEB's formula for determining exports would raise the presently projected figure for 1977 from 400 thousand barrels a day to 917 thousand barrels a day. (For a detailed exposition of how this higher figure is reached through the use of the NEB formula, see Appendix II).

It is likely that Canada has not seen the end of major oil exports to the U.S. Once the world oil price is reached, Canadians will be asked to accept higher export levels once again. After all, it will be much easier to bring Canadians around to accepting higher oil exports to the United States, provided they are already paying the world price, than it would be to convince them of the value of exports while the two-price system is in effect. That way, no easily visible connection between high oil prices for Canadians and high exports will exist.

A final word must be said on the subject of the drive of the oil companies first for higher prices based on low producibility estimates and later for new exports once the world price has been achieved. It has been assumed here that regarding the estimates of 1973 and 1974, it is the 1974 estimates that are low and not the 1973 estimates that are high. Some will agree that the oil companies misled the nation in one case or the other, but will argue that it is likelier that the 1973 estimate was the one that was wrong and that the 1974 estimate was a belated admission of the truth.

This is possible. Only access to oil companies' secret information could clarify the issue. It is also true that people close to the oil industry were saying in March 1975 that the companies had discovered vast oil reserves in the Canadian Arctic that they were not announcing until the federal government's royalty rates for the north had been established. But these remain rumours, nothing more. The problem is that although it is clear that the oil companies have misled the public, it is impossible to be certain in which direction they have done so.

This author's assessment is that the 1974 estimates involved a serious underestimate of Canadian producibility. This is based on the historic behaviour of the industry throughout the world. The oil industry has regularly resorted to the technique of underestimating reserves to force up prices and to force down the taxes they pay. In the 1920s, U.S. oil companies predicted that the United States would run out of domestic oil within five to ten years. Today, the U.S. has higher proven reserves than it had when these predictions were made half a century ago.

The classic problem of the oil industry has been glut, not shortage. This was the case internationally from 1950 to 1970 when the price of oil stayed exactly the same while the average price of commodities doubled. Again in 1975, the oil cartel and OPEC are faced with a renewed glut that threatens to break up the united front of the producing countries and to drive down the price of oil. [23]

In the Canadian case, it is very difficult to believe that the oil companies actually discovered a shortage at exactly the moment when it would most benefit them. Before 1973, the Canadian price was higher than the international price and there was no incentive for the companies to play the scarcity game. After the international price revolution, the world price was higher than the Canadian price. It was at that moment that the oil companies insisted that Canada faced shortages.

What this history of wildly fluctuating estimates demonstrates more than anything is the need for a reliable, independent source of information on oil resources, on which a sane Canadian energy policy can be based. We do not now have such information.

Who benefits from higher prices?

The oil companies have not set out to smash the two-price system in Canada simply to allow the federal and provincial governments to collect enormous new tax and royalty revenues. To get as much of the increased price as they can, the companies have battled fiercely to keep federal and provincial tax collectors at bay.

The target that drew the most concentrated fire of the oil industry was the May 1974 budget of Finance Minister John Turner. The budget, which came only a few weeks after the wellhead price of Canadian crude had been raised from $4.00 to $6.50 a barrel, made it clear that the federal government intended to fight the provinces for as large a share of oil royalties as it could get. The budget provided that the oil companies could no longer claim their provincial royalty payments as expenses against their federal taxes. At prices then prevailing, the Turner move would mean the collection of an additional billion dollars a year from the oil industry.[24]

The Turner measure was not simply designed to impose steep new taxes on the oil industry. It was designed to force the oil-producing provinces to lower their royalty rates, so that the federal government could, in effect, gain access to royalties for itself. When the oil companies protested that the new tax would ruin them, the federal finance minister invited them to seek respite from the governments of Alberta and Saskatchewan through the reduction of provincial royalty rates. It was a shrewd strategy for the finance minister to undertake. He knew that, in the end, the government of Alberta, with its total dependence on the petroleum industry, would retreat in the face of pressures from the corporations before Ottawa would.

A second measure in the Turner budget was more attractive to the oil industry: the provision that 70 per cent of the exploration expenses of the industry could be written off against federal taxes.[25]

The Turner budget provoked a storm of protest from the oil companies, the governments of Alberta and Saskatchewan and the federal Conservatives and NDP. It provided the federal Conservatives and NDP with the opportunity to merge forces to bring down the minority Liberal government.

Following their return to majority government in the July 1974 federal election, the Liberals were in a strong position to reintroduce their budgetary measures when the new Commons met in the fall. On November 18, John Turner brought down his second version of the controversial budget. It retained the measure for providing for non-deductibility of provincial royalty payments from federal taxes. But this budget was sweeter for the oil industry than the previous one. It extended the exploration expense write-off from 70 per cent to 100 per cent, a measure that gave the industry back an estimated $100 million in 1974 and that could amount to $185 million in 1975, according to the estimate of the *Financial Post*.[26]

Despite the finance minister's retreat, the petroleum industry responded to the budget with ferocious new threats of cutbacks in exploration activity. On November 29, 1974, J.A. Armstrong, Imperial Oil's chairman, sent out a letter to shareholders which complained about the heavy burden of taxation being borne by the oil industry. He wrote:

> The federal budget will have a major impact on the company's planned capital and exploration expenditures for 1975 and probably later years as well.
>
> The effect of the budget, combined with provincial tax and royalty levels, will be to reduce severely the company's available cash flow, and capital and exploration expenditures will of necessity be about $115 million less than had been originally budgeted for the coming year.
>
> The implications go far beyond the activities of Imperial Oil and the Canadian oil industry; they affect our country. If the tax objectives of the federal and provincial governments are not resolved in a way that lets the petroleum industry get on with the very large and costly job of developing new reserves, Canada will find itself deficient in domestic petroleum supply.

Armstrong concluded his patriotic letter by appealing to shareholders to write their federal and provincial elected members to urge them to get out of the oil industry's way.[27]

The financial press immediately trumpeted the oil industry's screams of gloom and doom. The *Financial Post* headlined the oil industry's reaction to the federal budget with a front-page story entitled, "Winddown begins for frustrated oil industry." The story began: "The Canadian oil industry, one of the fundamental economic forces in the country, seems about to blow its gasket."

The report went on to predict a significant downturn in exploration for new oil: "There is no doubt whatsoever in the minds of oil men that exploration and development activity will take a severe dip, beginning immediately and declining as current agreements between partners come to an end."[28]

Several pages later, the *Financial Post*, acting very much like a publicity front for the oil companies, painted a lurid picture of the stricken industry. The headline read: "Oil firms pull out their 'disaster' plans." The story reported that:

> Industry leaders predict without reservation that a significant slowdown in industrial activity will result.

Crisis signs include the flight of rigs and seismic crews from Alberta. The rigs leaving belong to Canadian companies, not to U.S. owners.

To sum up the situation: since Ottawa persisted and introduced a hard budget, Alberta will have to reach deep into its provincial bank holdings to keep its oil industry, still its major industry, alive.[29]

A few weeks later, almost as though the Premier of Alberta was starring in a melodrama, the *Financial Post* was delighted to report:

Well, Premier Lougheed has done it.

He has given in to pressure from Ottawa and demands from industry to lower his take from the oil industry.

The Premier, under pressure from the industry, backed down in the tax battle with Ottawa. He announced a new incentive programme, the Alberta Petroleum Exploration Plan, for the oil industry. Under the plan the province will refund to the oil companies a sum equal to the amount flowing to Alberta as a result of federal taxation of provincial royalties. In addition, Lougheed lowered the province's effective royalties on oil, from 40 per cent to 36 per cent on "old" oil (proven before the spring of 1974), and from 28 per cent to 27 per cent on "new" oil (proven after the spring of 1974).[30]

The oil industry estimated that the Premier's plan would place an additional $250 million to $300 million in their hands. Taking this sum together with Turner's refund of over $100 million, through his extension of the exploration expense write-off, the industry had managed to reduce the original increase in the tax bite from about one billion dollars a year to about $600 million between the time of Turner's budget of May 1974 and the end of the year.

When the oil companies announced their profits for 1974, their shareholders had reason to be proud of them for their efforts. The profits set records for corporate performance in Canada. Imperial Oil announced profits of $290 million for 1974, compared with $228 million for the year before.[31] Gulf's profits for the nine-month period ending September 30, 1974 were $128 million, a 92 per cent increase over the same period the year before when profits had been $67 million. Gulf's 92 per cent profit jump was recorded on the basis of a gross sales jump of only 39 per cent.[32] Shell's profits for the first nine months of 1974 almost doubled from $69 million to $119 million.[33]

However, the 1974 profit figures tell only a part of the story. The tax rollback means that as the price goes up to the world price in 1975 and 1976, the oil companies will get 40 per cent of the increase. Assuming that the price of oil reaches eleven dollars a barrel in 1976, the oil companies will get an additional two dollars a barrel. On Alberta's present proven reserve of about six billion barrels, the oil companies will get an additional $12 billion over the life of the reserve. This will be a straight addition to oil company profits, since present reserves were established on the basis of the old pricing system. The 1974 tax rollback guarantees the oil companies a $12-billion handout from the Canadian people — the biggest profit giveaway in Canadian history.

Syncrude: the prototype sellout

While the general campaign of the oil industry for higher prices and higher profits has been successful, its most significant achievement to date has been the winning of "new terms" for the Syncrude oil sands project. The showdown over Syncrude set important precedents for the future development of the Alberta oil sands and also for the development of Arctic oil and natural gas.

When the Conservative government of Peter Lougheed came to office in Alberta in 1971, it inherited the helter-skelter oil policies of its predecessor, the Social Credit Party. When Lougheed became premier, only one oil sands plant, the Great Canadian Oil Sands, a subsidiary of the Sun Oil Company of Pennsylvania, was in production.

Lougheed determined to establish order where chaos had formerly reigned. He commissioned Walter J. Levy, the New York oil consultant, to write a report for him on the development of the Alberta oil sands. Completed in February 1973, the report was entitled, *Emerging North American Oil Balances: Considerations Relevant to a Tar Sands Development Policy*.[34]

A reading of the Levy Report makes it easy to understand why its author was presented with a medal in 1968 by Dean Rusk, then U.S. secretary of state, in grateful appreciation for Levy's distinguished service to the United States. The Levy Report conceived of the development of the vast potential of the Alberta oil sands in strictly continental terms. The report outlined its general position as follows:

> From the standpoint of both U.S. and Canadian policies . . . there is an advantage to moving early and rapidly to develop tar sands production. For the United States, early development of the tar sands could contribute to the availability of secure North American oil supplies over the critical period before its own long-run efforts to develop continental and synthetic oil might begin to pay off. For Canada, the establishment of early and substantial volumes of tar sands production could be essential to maintenance of Canada's export potential, providing an offset to Canada's rising volumes of oil imports.[35]

Levy urged the province of Alberta to keep one jump ahead of the development of synthetic oil production elsewhere on the continent:

> The tar sands have already established an early lead over other North American synthetics in the development of technology and in experience with commercial-scale operations. Pushing ahead now could serve to maintain and perhaps even increase this lead. Alberta probably has the opportunity of developing second-generation plants by the time first-generation U.S. oil shale and coal liquification plants are coming onstream.[36]

Levy concluded that Alberta should seize the opportunity to help meet continental oil demand by pressing ahead with the oil sands:

> Alberta's huge tar sands offer a unique opportunity for the establishment of a major new industry, which could make a very valuable contribution both to North American oil requirements and to the province itself.[37]

Levy warned that Canada's potential for conventional crude oil production in the Prairies would peak in the late 1970s. Therefore, he concluded, the rapid development of the oil sands was essential to the maintenance of Canada's export potential.

In light of subsequent debates over the risks involved in oil sands ventures, the Levy Report's comments on profitability are significant:

> Over the longer-run . . . when technology and costs of tar sands production are reasonably well established, rates of return on investment in tar sands projects are likely to be closer to returns in manufacturing industries than to returns on *successful* exploration ventures. *Average* rates of return on tar sands projects should be reasonably comparable over the long run with average returns on total industry investment in conventional oil exploration/production, including both successes and the large number of exploratory failures.[38]

Armed with the advice of the Levy Report, including its recommendations that the multinational oil companies were the entities best suited to undertaking oil sand ventures, the Lougheed government proceeded to negotiate the establishment of major oil-sands production plants.

In September 1973, the government of Alberta signed an agreement with Syncrude Canada Ltd. to proceed with the development of an oil sands plant capable of producing 125,000 barrels of oil daily. Syncrude was a joint venture initially involving four American-owned oil companies: Imperial Oil, Cities Service Athabasca Inc., Atlantic Richfield Co. and Gulf Oil Canada Ltd.

In the fall of 1974, the Syncrude partners found the new fear of a domestic oil shortfall for Canada a convenient backdrop against which to act out their demand for better terms from government. When the project had first been unveiled by Premier Lougheed in September 1973 in an Alberta television spectacular, it had been called a one-billion-dollar undertaking. A year later the Syncrude partners said the old price tag was unrealistic; the project was going to cost two billion dollars. One of the partners, Atlantic Richfield Co., announced that the under-taking was getting too expensive and withdrew. The remaining partners in the Syncrude consortium issued an ultimatum: unless a new partner could be found and unless a billion dollars in new capital could be raised, the project would be abandoned. The consortium laid off work-ers at its job site near Fort McMurray in northeastern Alberta and cut its activities back to a bare minimum. Unless help was received from some quarter by the end of January 1975, Syncrude would go belly up, the companies said.

At the very end of the ultimatum period the Syncrude partners held a summit conference in Winnipeg with the president of Shell Oil Canada Ltd., the Premier of Alberta, Premier William Davis of Ontario, federal Minister of Energy Donald Macdonald, and Treasury Board President Jean Chretien. The conference started off with the president of Shell Canada Ltd. telling the others why his company would not participate in the venture. He left and the others carried on.

The conference ended with the announcement that the project had been saved. The Syncrude consortium had found three new investing partners — the federal government, the Alberta government and the Ontario government. The three governments announced that they were putting up $600 million: $300 million from the federal government, $200 million from Alberta and $100 million from Ontario. Later, questioning in the House of Commons disclosed that these sums were simply estimates of the extent of public investment. If, as the president of Imperial Oil indicated it might, the cost of the project rose still further, the public investment would increase. Macdonald told the Commons that the federal share estimated at $300 million was, in fact 15 per cent of the total cost of Syncrude, whatever that might be.[39]

Through their investment the three governments had become minor-ity partners in the joint venture. While not gaining control of the consortium, the three governments had effectively put up the working capital for its operations. What kind of return can the public expect for the massive investment it has now made in Syncrude?

Syncrude is a consortium, a joint venture, it is not a corporation in its own right. Majority control in the venture is vested in three American-owned oil companies. From their point of view, the object of the undertaking is to maximize their profits, not to declare high profits for Syncrude itself. Syncrude will be profitable to Imperial, Cities Service and Gulf through the pricing arrangements established between the consortium and the participating companies. It will be profitable because of the tax deductions the companies can make on the basis of the expenses of the consortium. When the consortium was first established in September 1973, Premier Lougheed announced to Albertans that the province would get half the profits from the venture. Syncrude's president, F.K. Spragins, a former Imperial Oil employee, said, however, that he did not expect the consortium to declare any profits at all for the first seven years of its operations.

From the viewpoint of the oil companies involved in Syncrude there is no reason why the consortium should ever declare a profit. That way the public investment will amount to an interest-free loan to the oil companies. The public will shoulder the burden of putting up the venture capital, but will get no monetary returns for its investment. In addition to its investment in Syncrude the federal government made two other decisions highly beneficial to the consortium. The government retreated from the Turner budget's decision to tax royalty payments to provincial governments in the case of Syncrude. This is a crucial decision because it will obviously serve as a precedent for future oil sands plants as well. As a larger and larger proportion of Canadian oil production comes from oil sands plants, this tax loophole will loom as an ever more important factor.

The federal government's second decision was the critical one: the concession to the consortium of the world price for its product. When Syncrude oil comes on stream in 1979, it will be sold at the going international price. For the oil industry as a whole, this federal government concession to Syncrude is a major victory in the battle to demolish the two-price system. Now that Syncrude has been allowed to make an end-run around the frozen Canadian price, the rest of the industry won't be far behind.

Syncrude can be expected to be only one of a series of oil sands ventures. At present, Petrofina and Home Oil are also considering oil sands undertakings.[40]

The natural-gas shortage scare and the Arctic

The petroleum industry's downward revision of its oil producibility estimates have been paralleled by a similar downward revision of its estimates of natural gas producibility. A gas shortage scare has developed which is creating tremendous pressure for quick government approval of schemes to build pipelines to transport Arctic gas to southern markets. The gas scare is the key factor in the current approach of the federal government to the development of both gas and oil reserves in the Canadian North.

A brief review of the evolution of the nation's natural gas industry since 1970 demonstrates the same shift from optimism to pessimism as in the case of oil. Again, late 1973, the period of the international oil-price revolution, is the pivotal period in the industry's change of view.

In 1970 the major gas exporting companies made applications to the NEB to export over 9 trillion cubic feet of natural gas to the United States. The gas companies were publicly indignant when the NEB approved the export of only two-thirds of the amount sought, 6.3 trillion cubic feet. The industry protested that Canada's natural gas reserves were sufficiently large to justify the full export. Again, in the fall of 1971, the gas companies were indignant when the NEB refused to allow a further extension of gas exports.

In its June 1973 energy report, the Department of Energy, Mines and Resources estimated Canada's proven reserves of natural gas as equivalent to a twenty-three-year supply at the 1972 level of production.[41] In addition, the report projected the existence of a further probable fifteen-year supply of natural gas in the Prairies at the 1972 level of production.

The energy report's optimistic estimates made it appear that Canada could easily meet its domestic demand for natural gas, as well as its export commitments, from its reserves in the prairie provinces until the end of the 1980s. But this optimism concerning natural gas disappeared during the same months as the petroleum industry was scaling down its estimates of Canada's oil producibility. In the winter of 1974, the Canadian Petroleum Association warned the federal government that Canada could run short of natural gas in the early 1980s. The CPA warned the government that Arctic supplies of natural gas would be urgently needed by the end of the 1970s, if the nation was to avoid a shortfall.

The NEB followed the shift of the petroleum industry with respect to natural gas in the same way as it had with oil. In March 1973, NEB Vice-Chairman Douglas Fraser had stated, "We see the proven gas reserves we now have before us as being ample to cover Canadian deliverability requirements up to the end of the eighties, or into the early nineties." In May 1974, NEB Chairman Marshall Crowe said, "It is now evident that shortages of gas supply will appear before the end of this decade."[42]

Despite the NEB's tendency to follow the industry from one set of estimates to another, some public officials were becoming skeptical about the self-serving nature of the new estimates. A Canadian Press story quoted one official of the federal Department of Energy, Mines and Resources as having said, "You sometimes get the feeling they send their engineers and geologists to the hearing to give the statistical information to support whatever they are looking for."[43]

On March 21, 1974, Canadian Arctic Gas Pipe Line Ltd. made application to the NEB to build a natural gas pipeline to supply American and Candian markets with Alaskan and Canadian Arctic gas. The Company was acting on behalf of the gas consortium, Canadian Arctic Gas Study Ltd., which, as mentioned in Chapter 10, includes a powerful corporate line-up — Imperial Oil Ltd., Gulf Oil Canada Ltd., Shell Canada Ltd. and Canadian Pacific Investments Ltd.[44] The application to construct the pipeline concluded several years of intense corporate and government activity in building support for the project. By the time the application was made, several ministers in the federal Liberal government had been on record for two years in support of the pipeline.

By the fall of 1974, the mighty gas consortium was faced with a smaller Canadian rival, the proposed Maple Leaf Line, promoted by Alberta Gas Trunk Lines Ltd. The Maple Leaf Line would transport only Canadian gas to Canadian markets. It would involve a 42-inch pipeline rather than the 48-inch line proposed by its larger rival. Proponents of the Maple Leaf Line claim they could complete the project for just over three billion dollars, less than half the current estimates for building the joint Canadian-American line.[45]

Rivalry between the two pipeline proposals is not the central issue however. The pressure for Arctic gas is related to the existing commitment of half of Canadian gas production to the U.S. through long-term contracts. Canada at present produces about two trillion cubic feet of natural gas annually. Even based on the petroleum industry's new lower gas estimates, without these exports neither gas pipeline would be needed to meet Canadian needs before the 1990s.

Coming fast on the heels of schemes to build gas pipelines from the Arctic is a proposal from the major oil companies for a Mackenzie Valley oil pipeline. Dubbed an "all Canadian" venture (because it would ship only Canadian and not Alaskan oil) the participants include Imperial Oil, Gulf Oil Canada Ltd., Shell Canada Ltd., Interprovincial Pipe Line Ltd. and Trans Mountain Pipe Line Co. Ltd.[46]

These proposals for pipelines to transport Arctic gas and oil are and will be the subject matter of various government hearings during 1975. The Mackenzie Valley pipeline is being considered by Mr. Justice Thomas Berger in Yellowknife, N.W.T., in a hearing that began on March 4, 1975. NEB hearings to consider the projects are expected in the fall of 1975.

Despite the hearings, the government continues to make its preference clear — the building of both natural gas and oil pipelines in the Mackenzie Valley as joint Canadian-American ventures. In a statement in the House of Commons on February 7, 1975, Energy Minister Donald Macdonald explained that in addition to the government's support for the Mackenzie Valley pipeline, "we have under active consideration with American officials now the question of whether there is a possibility of developing an oil pipeline as well, to link the resources from United States sources in Alaska with those now being developed in the Mackenzie Valley."[47]

The intense pressure to go ahead with Arctic pipelines for gas and oil (possibly before the Berger hearings are over, as Mitchell Sharp hinted in the Commons on March 4, 1975), grows out of the new, lower estimates of Canadian producibility that have been developed by the petroleum industry. With respect to natural gas, the petroleum industry either misled the NEB as to the prospects of gas production when it sought additional exports in 1970 and 1971, or it was misleading the NEB in 1974 when it claimed that Canada would need Arctic gas by the end of the 1970s.

The estimates of gas producibility put forward by the petroleum industry during the optimistic years resulted in long-term Canadian commitments to export about one-half of Canadian gas production through the seventies and eighties. If the new projection of shortages for Canada is accurate, it means that Canadians will be forced to rely on Arctic gas, two or three times as costly to produce as prairie gas, about a decade sooner than would have been the case with no exports.

Moreover, in the case of natural gas, it is more difficult to phase out exports than it is with oil. This is because gas exports have been agreed to through long-term contracts, while oil has been exported on a month-to-month basis. Expensive pipeline systems have been constructed in the United States to carry the Canadian gas.

Under the NEB Act the federal government has the authority to curtail exports that have been planned on the basis of incorrect information regarding gas reserves. In the winter of 1975, Energy Minister Macdonald warned the Americans that he might make use of this escape clause and might cut back on gas exports if he felt this was necessary to meet Canadian demand. The hint of possible export cutbacks led to a highly publicized American threat of economic retaliation. In an exclusive story, Ross Munro, the *Globe and Mail*'s Washington correspondent, reported that State Department officials had told him the United States was considering counteraction if the gas exports were cut back. The retaliation mentioned to Munro was the possible curtailment of coal exports to Canada that supply the Canadian steel industry. [48] The export question will be settled by the NEB in the spring of 1975 when new hearings on Canada's natural gas reserves are completed.

Whichever way the NEB rules on exports, the main effect of the gas supply scare has been to fuel the petroleum industry's campaign for higher gas prices and for quick action to proceed with an Arctic pipeline.

Politically, the Arctic gas and oil proposals are proceeding in very much the same way as the Syncrude project. An atmosphere of apprehension concerning potential gas and oil shortages is providing the industry with an ideal climate in which to press for favourable royalty rates, taxation policies and direct investments by government to assist with pipeline ventures. A future showdown, very much like the Syncrude summit in Winnipeg, is on the agenda.

The future of Canadian energy policy

The major petroleum companies have removed most of the political obstacles blocking them from imposing the world price of oil on Canadians. Canadians will pay the world price, but it will not be because the federal government has made an independent assessment of the nation's oil producibility that concludes that this price is needed to guarantee adequate production for the future. It is the oil industry that has supplied the figures. Government agencies, established to regulate the industry, are forced to accede to the industry's assessments because these agencies have no independent means to make an overall estimate. That the National Energy Board has done little more than follow the petroleum industry from one set of production estimates to another is evident from the NEB's behaviour in 1973 and 1974. Far from regulating the industry, the NEB has ended up as a front office for it.

In the spring of 1975, the Canadian price of crude oil will climb to at least $8.50 a barrel, on the way to reaching the world price a year later. The price of gasoline will increase about ten cents a gallon with each of the two increases. Naturally, other fuels, including heating oil and natural gas, will experience equivalent price increases. The price rise will result in a jump of one full point on the consumer price index in the spring of 1975 and again a year later.

The companies have not only succeeded in winning the battle for higher prices, they have also won the battle to appropriate about 40 per cent of the price increase for their production of conventional crude oil in western Canada. This is the result of their successful war with Ottawa and the provincial governments in 1974. The 40 per cent of the coming price increase will be pure gravy for the industry, since the oil that is being produced was made available through exploration and development expenditures made before the new price structure came into effect.

The old price structure guaranteed the companies considerable profit. The new price structure hands them enormous windfall profits, amounting to an additional twelve billion dollars over the life of Alberta's present crude oil reserves.

While the companies have done well in increasing their returns on conventional oil production, they have done even better in establishing a favourable climate for themselves in the development of the oil sands and frontier oil and natural gas. The Syncrude deal provided them with three crucial and highly profitable precedents: huge public investments of venture capital (without public control of the venture), a full-scale retreat of the federal government on taxing policy (Syncrude can write off its royalty payments against federal taxes), and the concession of the world price for Syncrude's products. The Syncrude settlement will serve as the model for future oil-sands plants and for oil and gas developments in the Arctic.

Once the world price for petroleum has been achieved, the oil companies will likely further their own interests by proclaiming the discovery of new reserves that put the country back into a surplus position.

Canada's potential petroleum reserves remain large and the oil industry's temptation to use them to feed American markets remains as high as ever in a political climate of increasing insecurity for the oil companies in the Middle East and in Africa. As a resource base, Canada is still the safe backyard of the United States, compared with any other foreign source.

The imposition of the world monopoly price of energy on Canada and the continuing push toward continental integration of energy development, distorts the Canadian economy. Monopoly energy prices have already been a major contributing factor in creating the worst recession the western world has experienced since the 1930s. The recession which has been spilling over into Canada from the United States is the immediate context within which Canadian resource and industrial strategies are being formulated.

A general crisis of surplus industrial capacity in relation to available markets is the problem facing all advanced western countries. The crisis has been most evident in consumer durable industries like the automobile industry and electrical products. In these industries western countries have faced depression-level unemployment.

In January 1975, U.S. unemployment stood at 8.2 per cent and American industry was operating at less than 75 per cent capacity. Hard times for American industry and severe competition between the United States and the other leading industrial nations, the western European countries and Japan, have forced the United States to seek rationalized relationships with dependent countries like Canada.

The United States can no longer afford the luxury of a special relationship with its wealthiest dependency. Canada is a critical source of resources for the United States and is a key market for American manufactured goods. In 1974, Canadian imports of manufactured goods per capita were unparalleled in the history of industrial countries. Canadians ended up with a $9-billion deficit in trade in manufactured products. In the single case of the automobile industry, our deficit was $1.5 billion, $950 million of which was with the United States. After a decade of the auto pact we have returned to steeper deficits than we had before the pact was concluded.

In the early months of 1975 many Canadians were inclined to regard their problems as relatively light in relation to those of other industrialized countries. American unemployment was higher than ours. The recession was hitting the United States harder than it was hitting Canada. But, in fact, Canada has been following the American economy into the recession. The recession has developed in the United States as capital expenditures have fallen off in manufacturing industries. The Canadian economy as a supplier of raw materials is being affected as American manufacturers lessen their demand for Canadian raw products. The first impact of the recession in Canada has been in the manufacturing centres, with Ontario experiencing a very rapid increase in unemployment. As the recession deepens, it spreads to the resource-producing regions of the country through a falling off in capital investment in resource industries. A downturn in investment in resource industries affects the Canadian economy as basically as downturn in manufacturing investments affects the United States.

Faced with recession and growing rates of unemployment, Canadian politicians will be inclined to look for resource development projects that can keep the economy moving. This has always been the response of Canadian governments to the problems of a branch-plant economy during hard economic times.

The government defended the Syncrude deal, in part, by the need to keep up employment levels in Alberta's petroleum industry. Future deals will be justified in the same way. And in recessionary times, the corporations are often wary about putting up their own venture capital; they prefer, if possible, to seek government outlays of public capital in joint ventures in which the corporations retain control and appropriate most of the benefits. The Syncrude deal will serve as a prototype for the financing of resource projects during the recession.

The problem of energy policy is an aspect of the problem of establishing an independent Canadian industrial strategy. Although the battle for Canadian independence, for new resource and industrial strategies has influenced a large proportion of Canadians, it has scarcely begun to influence organized politics in Canada.

Energy policy in Canada continues to be formulated in a political context that remains basically continentalist. Evidence of the continentalist bias of Canadian politics was the absence of effective political opposition to the Syncrude deal despite the overwhelming cynicism displayed by Canadians concerning its announcement. And Syncrude was followed a few weeks later by remarkable evidence of the continentalist bias of the economic advice given to governments in Canada. The Toronto *Star* reported that all twenty-four members of the Economic Council of Canada were in support of a report, about to be submitted, that favours complete free trade between Canada and the United States.[49]

Canada urgently needs a new set of energy policies that are developed in harmony with an industrial strategy. Before such a policy can be intelligently formulated, Canadians have to put an end to the effective monopoly of information concerning the nation's petroleum potential enjoyed by the oil companies. The ability of the petroleum industry to change the thinking of the nation about its energy potential in the space of sixteen months is an awesome example of propaganda power.

The disparity between the estimates of producibility of petroleum published in the energy reports of 1973 and 1974 are so shocking that a full-scale investigation into the reasons for the downward revision of forecasts should be carried out by a public inquiry. A board of inquiry with broad powers to subpoena the records of the petroleum companies should be established by the federal government. To be credible, such a board should include critics of the petroleum industry and representatives of popular organizations, like trade unions or teachers' associations. A board which included critics of the oil industry like Eric Kierans, Mel Hurtig, Ian McDougall or Mel Watkins would give the public confidence that they were not being treated to a snow job. Among other things such a board should investigate the relationship between the petroleum companies and government regulatory bodies like the NEB.

An inquiry could provide Canadians with data on which to plan an energy policy geared to Canada's needs. It could assess the proper level of investment in energy projects for the next decade. It could determine in a rational manner the proper price for petroleum products, by establishing a price based on the cost of production, plus the cost of replacing present reserves, plus the cost of research into new forms of energy for the longer run. Such a pricing formula would give Canadians both an assurance of energy supplies for the long term and the benefit of the lowest possible energy prices for consumers and for industry. While it is difficult to estimate in advance what such a price would be, it certainly would be far below the world monopoly price of eleven dollars a barrel for crude oil.

Such a pricing policy is critical in the formulation of an industrial strategy for Canada. It would give the nation the benefit of the cheapest possible fuel costs while not making Canada a pollution haven, industrialized through the too-rapid depletion of its natural resources. There can be no doubt that an energy price that stands below the world level will assist Canada considerably in making the transition to an independent industrial economy.

Even without an inquiry much is already clear: the nation should commit itself for the long term to the husbanding of Canadian petroleum reserves for Canadian needs. We should substitute a ban on oil exports for the current export formula which would allow the oil companies to expand exports on the basis of new estimates of producibility, once the world price is achieved in Canada.

In the case of natural gas, urgent action along the same lines is required. The reason Canada is being pressed into the development of expensive Arctic gas in the 1970s is that the oil industry recommended vast exports on the basis of optimistic estimates of gas supply in the Prairies. If, as the industry now claims, the Prairies cannot meet the domestic and export demand, it follows that the earlier estimates were false. In that case, the federal government has the power under the National Energy Board Act to eliminate the exports and to husband prairie reserves for domestic use. Such an action would postpone the need for an expensive Mackenzie Valley gas pipeline until the end of the 1980s.

Finally, the record of the foreign-owned petroleum industry in Canada makes it clear that the present owners of the industry will always use their control of an indispensable industrial resource to blackmail the nation into going along with their demands. It should be evident by now that only when the oil industry is made a public utility, owned by the provincial and federal governments, can we develop a resource policy that is in the interest of Canadian consumers and industries. Such a policy could serve as the first step in a new industrial strategy in which Canadian resources can be used as the basis for creating industrial jobs in Canada.

In the longer term it will take socialist economic policies and a formidable political struggle for the Canadian people to achieve independence. Right now, though, what is needed is an alliance of all Canadian nationalists who are opposed to the present course of energy policy in Canada. At present the oil companies and the Canadian Petroleum Association are organized into a lobby whose power has never been equalled in this country. Before it is too late for the present course to be altered, Canadian nationalists should organize an effective opposition to the oil industry.

Appendix I

The NEB report arrived at its conclusion that Canada should cut back on exports to the United States, but not eliminate them altogether, on the basis of the following criteria. The report states:

> On the basis of the supply and demand data set forth it is readily seen that a deficiency of supply to meet the Canadian demand for feedstocks from indigenous oil is possible in the early 1980s.
> . . . In view of this foreseeable deficiency, the Board recognizes the natural desire to conserve remaining reserves through the reduction or elimination of exports. On the other hand, it recognizes such a measure would only be effective for a short period and that the best protection in the long run is obtained from an active, and economically healthy industry, continually increasing the available energy materials. The cost of finding and producing new reserves will be significantly higher than the cost of reserves added during the last two decades. A large reduction in current producing rates would deprive industry of one of its sources of cash-flow required to find these higher cost reserves, as well as idling a portion of the capacity of producing facilities which have been financed over the past few years. . . . If exports were immediately discontinued the Board believes that reserve addition rates would be no more than one-half of those that would be forthcoming if new reserves were to have immediate market access. Using this assumption . . . an immediate cessation of exports would delay a supply-demand intersection by 2.6 years. . . . On balance it is the Board's opinion that the disruptive effect of an immediate cessation of all exports would not be in the best interests of Canada in terms of securing long term energy supplies.
> At the other extreme, the Board does not agree with those submittors who say that no protection formula is required.[1]

With this reasoning the NEB concluded that Canada should decide on the appropriate level of oil exports with the aid of a formula that would involve some protection of Canadian reserve capacity. The report outlined a set of criteria for the establishment of such a formula. Included in the criteria were these considerations:

> It should be sufficiently flexible to respond to changing oil supply-demand circumstances, to emergence of new oil supply sources and to changing economics.

It should provide incentive and encouragement to the industry by permitting some proportion of *increased* production potential to be reflected in increased production rates.

The percentage reduction in exports should be increasingly severe if and as the supply-demand intersection approaches. This would give industry the greatest possible incentive in early years to take steps to avert the shortfall.[2]

The formula arrived at in the report was expressed in a simple equation:

$$E = [P - (D + C)]t/10$$

(*t* not to exceed 10)

The terms in the equation were defined as follows:

E is the annual average volume in thousands of barrels per day available for export licensing during the year for which the determination is made.

P is the forecast annual average potential producibility of crude oil and equivalent in thousands of barrels per day during the year for which the determination is made.

D is the forecast annual average demand for Canadian use in thousands of barrels per day for western Canadian crude oil and equivalent during the year for which the determination is made.

C is the forecast total increase that would have occurred in demand for western Canadian crude oil and equivalent in thousands of barrels per day if conservation measures had not been effective.

t is the time during which supply is forecast to exceed Canadian demand, from January 1 of the year for which the determination is made, expressed to the nearest one-tenth of a year, and extended to a maximum of ten years.[3]

Later in the report the equation was used as the basis for establishing the allowable levels of exports for 1975. Canadian demand for domestic crude included oil demand west of the Ottawa Valley plus 250 thousand barrels a day for the Montreal market. The equation was applied as follows:

$$E = [P - (D + C)]t/10$$
$$E = [2100 - (1205 + 0)] \ 7.3/10$$
$$E = 653 \text{ thousand barrels a day.}[4]$$

Appendix II

To demonstrate how easily the export phase out programme can be reversed by greater optimism concerning producibility based on higher domestic prices, let us construct a hypothetical scenario. If, instead of using the forecasts for producibility for 1982 selected by the NEB in its October 1974 report, we use instead the highest estimates submitted by the oil industry for Canadian producibility in that year, we get very different results. This is not an unreasonable thing to do, considering that the most optimistic estimates made to the NEB in 1974 were far more pessimistic than the most pessimistic estimates made to the Department of Energy, Mines and Resources in 1973.

Using these more optimistic estimates, Canadian crude oil producibility in 1982 would be 1590 thousand barrels a day from conventional sources, 505 thousand barrels a day from the oil sands and 200 thousand barrels a day from the Arctic. Instead of 1510 thousand barrels a day in 1982 (the figure the report settled on), the level of potential producibility would be 2295 thousand barrels a day. Leaving the figure for Canadian demand from domestic sources the same as that in the report, 1530 thousand barrels a day, the projected shortfall would not take place in 1982. Instead Canada would continue to have surplus producing capacity in that year.

Let us suppose further that Richardson Securities and other observers are correct in forecasting that the Canadian domestic crude oil price will reach the world price level in 1976. It is quite possible that later in 1976, the oil industry will return to the NEB with new forecasts, much like the one above.

How then would the export allotment for 1977 be affected? Again using the most optimistic forecasts presented to the NEB, let us make use of the agency's formula. Traditional conventional production would amount to 2187 thousand barrels a day. In order to make the forecast more plausible, let us accept the higher figure for conventional producibility but stick with the lower NEB estimate for oil sands output; 65 thousand barrels a day. This would put Canadian producibility for 1977 at 2252 thousand barrels a day, while Canadian demand for Canadian crude would be 1285 thousand barrels a day, and conservation measures would have saved 50 thousand barrels a day.

Having determined that with our new estimates for 1982, Canadian producibility would remain in excess of Canadian demand for domestic crude, no supply-demand intersection could be foreseen in the next ten years, the Board's maximum allowable time-frame. Let us now make use of the NEB's formula in arriving at an export level for 1977:

$$E = [P - (D + C)]\, t/10$$
$$E = [2252 - (1285 + 50)]\ 10/10$$
$$E = 917 \text{ thousand barrels a day}[1]$$

With our scenario, exports to the United States would amount to 917 thousand barrels a day instead of the NEB's projection of 400 thousand barrels a day.

Notes

[1]Canada, Department of Energy, Mines and Resources report, *An Energy Policy for Canada—Phase I* (Ottawa, Department of Energy, Mines and Resources, 1973), v. 1, p. 40.

[2]Pierre Trudeau, *Notes for the Prime Minister's Statement on National T.V., November 22, 1973* (Ottawa, Office of the Prime Minister, 1973).

[3]Canada, Department of Energy Report, *op. cit.*, v. 1, pp. 102, 103.

[4]*Globe and Mail*, January 4, 1974.

[5]*Ibid.*, January 4, 1974.

[6]*Financial Post*, March 25, 1974.

[7]National Energy Board, *Report to the Honourable Minister of Energy, Mines and Resources in the Matters of the Exportation of Oil* (Ottawa, Information Canada, 1974).

[8]Canada, Department of Energy Report, *op. cit.*, v. 1, p. 104.

[9]National Energy Board, *op. cit.*, pp. Appendix 2-i, 2-iii.

[10]*Ibid.*, p. Appendix 3-v.

[11]*Ibid.*, p. Appendix 3-v.

[12]*Ibid.*, p. 2-13.

[13]*Ibid.*, p. Appendix 4-iv.

[14]*Financial Post*, December 1, 1974.

[15]Economic Council of Canada, *Eleventh Annual Report* (Ottawa, 1974), pp. 191, 236, 237.

[16]*Financial Post*, February 8, 1975.

[17]*Financial Post*, February 15, 1975.

[18]Canada, Department of Energy Report, *op. cit.*, v. 1, p. 90.

[19]National Energy Board, *op. cit.*, p. 2-14.

[20]Richardson Securities of Canada, *Economic Comments*, January 15, 1975.

[21]Canada, *House of Commons Debates*, Friday, February 7, 1975, p. 3020.

[22]*Ibid.*, p. 3020.

[23]*The Economist*, February 15, 1975.

[24]*Financial Post*, December 14, 1974.

[25]*Ibid.*, October 19, 1974.

[26]*Ibid.*, December 14, 1974.

[27]J. A. Armstrong, *Imperial Oil Limited letter to stockholders*, November 29, 1974.

[28]*Financial Post*, December 1, 1974.

[29]*Ibid.*, December 14, 1974.

[30]*Ibid.*, December 14, 1974.

[31]Data card for Imperial Oil Ltd., February 13, 1975, compiled by the Financial Post Corporation Service, Toronto.

[32]Data card for Gulf Oil Ltd., February 6, 1975, compiled by the Financial Post Corporation Service, Toronto.

[33]Data card for Shell Canada Ltd., February 4, 1975, compiled by the Financial Post Corporation Service, Toronto.

[34]W. J. Terry, *Emerging North American Oil Balances: Considerations Relevant to a Tar Sands Development Policy* (Edmonton, 1973).

[35]*Ibid.*, p. vii.

[36]*Ibid.*, p. xi.

[37]*Ibid.*, p. xiv.

[38]*Ibid.*, p. iv-2.

[39]Canada, *House of Commons Debates*, Friday, February 7, 1975, p. 3019.

[40]*Ibid.*, p. 3021.

[41]Canada, Department of Energy Report, *op. cit.*, v. 1, p. 42.

[42]*Weekend Magazine*, March 1, 1975.

[43]*Edmonton Journal*, March 11, 1975.

[44]Data card for Imperial Oil Ltd., September 4, 1974, compiled by the Financial Post Corporation Service, Toronto.

[45]*Weekend Magazine*, March 1, 1975.

[46]Data card for Imperial Oil Ltd., February 13, 1975, compiled by the Financial Post Corporation Service, Toronto.

[47]Canada, *House of Commons Debates*, Friday, February 7, 1975, p. 3020.

[48]*Globe and Mail*, February 6, 1975.

[49]*Toronto Star*, February 11, 1975.

Appendix I
Notes

[1] National Energy Board, *op cit.*, pp. 4-3, 4-4, 4-5.
[2] *Ibid.*, pp. 4-6, 4-7.
[3] *Ibid.*, pp. 4-8, 4-9.
[4] *Ibid.*, p. Appendix 4-iv.

Appendix II
Notes

[1] National Energy Board, *op cit.*, p. Appendix 2-1.